KINGDOM WORKS

TRUE STORIES ABOUT GOD AND HIS PEOPLE IN INNER CITY AMERICA

BART CAMPOLO

VINE BOOKS

SERVANT PUBLICATIONS
ANN ARBOR, MICHIGAN

Vine Books is an imprint of Servant Publications especially designed to serve evangelical Christians.

Although the men and women whose stories are told in this book are real, their names have been changed to protect the privacy of those involved.

Published by Servant Publications
P.O. Box 8617
Ann Arbor, Michigan 48107

Cover design: Paul Higdon

Photography: Owen Brock, Michael Wilson

01 02 03 04 10 9 8 7 6 5 4 3 2

Printed in the United States of America
ISBN 1-56955-195-2

LIBRARY OF CONGRESS CATALOGING-IN-PUBICATION DATA

Campolo, Bart.
    Kingdom Works: true stories about God and his people in inner city America / Bart Campolo.
        p. cm.
    ISBN 1-56955-195-2 (alk. paper)
    1. City missions—United States—Case studies. 2. Church work with the poor—United States—Case studies. I. Title.

BV2765 .C36 2000
277.3'0829'091732—dc21

                                                    00-065431

DEDICATION

To Andy Nolan, godfather of my children,
who gardens the city and keeps the faith.

CONTENTS

FOREWORD

The author of this book is my son—and I am very proud of him! With his gifts, education, and personal charisma (I am sure there is some fatherly prejudice in this evaluation of him), he could be earning a small fortune in the corporate world. Instead, he has chosen to create a ministry called Mission Year.

Bart has used his considerable skills as a speaker on college campuses and at various youth gatherings to challenge hundreds of men and women between eighteen and twenty-nine years of age to live counter to the pervasive narcissistic consumption-crazy lifestyles prescribed by our culture. He has called them to give up at least a year to live out a dangerous gospel in dangerous neighborhoods. Teams of visionaries he has recruited follow the radical directives of Jesus (see Matthew 10) in Atlanta, Georgia; Philadelphia, Pennsylvania; Chicago, Illinois; and Oakland, California. They are going door to door in the neighborhoods where they have been sent to serve, meeting people and blessing them. They are working as fellow servants with people who run soup kitchens, tutor at-risk children, and build decent housing for poor families. They are being friends to teenagers who have lost their dreams. They are visiting widows who have become prisoners in their own homes.

I believe that Bart has found something in Generation X that most of us have overlooked. He has discovered in them a latent idealism that is waiting to be formed into a strong movement—a movement that could have transforming effects on our nation. Bart has recognized many in this youthful cohort who long to do something heroic with their lives. What gave birth to Mission Year was Bart's desire to provide a vehicle through which the heroic idealism of these young people could be expressed in Christian ministry.

Since childhood Bart has been aware that the essence of Christianity is not so much to defend a dogmatic theology as it is to serve with a living Jesus who is waiting to be embraced by those in need. When Bart was just ten years old, I took him with me to the slums of Santo Domingo in the Dominican Republic and I saw how he related with kindness to the impoverished children who lived there. Before he was out of high school, Bart was involved in ministries to the poor in Philadelphia and Camden, New Jersey. During his years as a student at Haverford College and at Brown University, Bart was always more interested in working with socially disinherited children and teenagers than in getting involved with school-sponsored extracurricular activities. Later, I observed with great satisfaction as my son adopted as his motto for life: "Love God. Love people. Nothing else matters." Bart has grown up to be a man who recognizes that the Jesus he loves not only calls us to meet the needs of others, but has designed us so that there can be no meaning to our lives unless we do. Mission Year is the embodiment of that truth.

As you read this book, I hope you will get to know something of the son I know and love. The stories he writes are expressions of who and what Bart is. The young missionaries he writes about do what they do because they have heard the call to radical discipleship as Bart preaches it. His is a biblically based message full of adventure. And what Mission Year is doing is truly remarkable.

I hope that the stories told here will touch your heart and elicit compassion. I hope that through them you will get a glimpse of the paths of many urban dwellers who live in what Michael Harrington called "The Other America." And I pray that what you read will inspire you to step out and do something for others, even as my son Bart and his missionaries have done.

Tony Campolo
Eastern College
St. Davids, Pennsylvania

ONE

Dreams of Glory

When I was in seventh grade, my basketball coach used to take our team up to the high school to watch varsity games. There, in the excitement of the crowd, he made sure we soaked in the atmosphere. We got programs and ate hot dogs. We clapped with the pep band and fell in love with the cheerleaders. Most of all, we watched our heroes battle for glory and cheered for them like crazy. And always, at some point, our coach would turn to us and ask, "Do you like it up here, boys? Of course you do! Well, now you know what you're shooting for, and why we work so hard. We've got to get you ready, because one day that's going to be you out there in the big time!"

My coach was no fool. He knew that young people could be motivated by dreams of glory. He knew that, given a truly exciting and very concrete vision for our near future, my teammates and I would practice hard and play our hearts out to make it happen. And so we did.

Frankly, after years of preaching radical discipleship to Christian young people, I am convinced that for the most part preaching radical discipleship doesn't work. No matter how good our message may be, the fact is that most kids simply cannot visualize what we are talking about. The problem is not that they are unwilling to become true followers of Jesus. The problem is that they do not know what following Jesus really means. Those kids need dreams of glory. They need an exciting and very concrete vision for the near future. They need to see a varsity game, so to speak, to experience what the "big-time" of radical discipleship is all about.

In my own Christian life, that varsity game has been outreach ministry and community development in some of this country's toughest inner-city neighborhoods. Like many urban missionaries, I first came to the city as a freshly converted teenager, full of enthusiasm but without a clue as to what it might mean for me to truly follow Jesus. I loved being part of my youth group and was fanatically devoted to propagating the fundamental theology I learned there, but my own relationship with God had hardly begun to develop. In other words, I had the kind of faith that seldom survives college.

In the city, however, God became real to me. Perhaps because both good and evil were so much easier to identify, I got caught up in the battle. I was just a day-camp counselor, but that was enough. My kids were poor. Some were hungry, some were abused. I met drug dealers, prostitutes, and homeless men who were utterly lost, and I wanted to help them. I met pastors and community leaders who were strong and courageous, and I wanted to be like them. Suddenly radical discipleship was more than a moral code and a new circle of friends. It was a total commitment to outreach, loving relationships, and social justice. And so, in a whole new way, Jesus became my hero.

He still is, of course. The longer I live and work among the poor, the more I love Jesus. And the more I love Jesus, the more convinced I am that we must send our young people to live and work among the poor. I am not talking about week-long mission trips, either, good though they may be. I am talking about the kind of serious time and real sacrifice that makes room for genuine relationships and changed neighborhoods. I am talking about Mission Year.

Simply stated, Mission Year recruits Christian young people eighteen to twenty-nine years of age from all over North America to join teams that live and work together in a poor urban neighborhood as "members" of a strong local church, reaching out to love their neighbors in a variety of practical ways. Besides church participation, these young people's weekly routine is devoted to community service (in public schools, hospitals, shelters, and other agencies) and neighborhood outreach, along with ongoing ministry training, team building, and daily personal devotions. This is street-level stuff, with a real premium on learning how to build authentic relationships for the sake of the kingdom of God.

The following stories and reflections have all either come out of or gone into my ongoing work with Mission Year. Though it has gone by different names, that work has always been about mobilizing and equipping young people to help build the kingdom of God here in the inner city. As I hope you will see, often those young people are the ones most changed by their efforts.

Indeed, as far as I am concerned, Mission Year is that varsity game our kids need to see. Here is a cutting-edge nationwide program that asks for and gets an incredible amount of commitment out of all kinds of Christian young people. Here is a vital movement that effectively combines spiritual growth, relational evangelism, and meaningful social action into the kind of radical discipleship that preachers like me can never really put into words. Here is something so real and powerful that a youthworker can point to it and say, "You like that, young people? Of course you do! Well, now you know what you're shooting for, and why we work so hard. We've got to get you ready, because one day that's going to be you out there in the big-time!"

The Mormons figured out all this stuff a long time ago. We may not like their theology, but we Christians must respect the commitment of Mormon young people. They are out there, year in and year out, more than fifty thousand strong, knocking on doors all over the world. Every Mormon grows up expecting to serve for at least two years. I believe the time has come for every Christian young person to grow up—and to be trained up—expecting to serve as well, in Mission Year or something like it.

The job of the church is not just to get our young people through high school and college safe and sound, but to make them into radical disciples of Jesus Christ, ready, willing, and able to transform this world into the kingdom of God. We will not lose them because we ask too much. We will lose them if we keep asking too little. Now is the time to give them exciting and concrete visions of what they can do and who they can become! Now is the time to give them dreams of glory!

TWO

A Simple Request

Imagine an inner-city neighborhood. The houses are old and worn out. The streets are dirty. Noise is everywhere: traffic, rap music, laughter, arguments, kids. Lots and lots of kids.

Now imagine a houseful of young people living in that neighborhood as disciples of Jesus. People who seek out their neighbors, listen to their needs, and pray for them over and over. People who work hard to make things better. People who stay long enough to become good friends.

Imagine those young people living simply, setting aside material comforts for the sake of spiritual growth and loving relationships. Imagine that house becoming a haven, a safe and accepting place where people see the gospel lived out, alive and available to all. Imagine each individual in that house getting up early each day to listen to God, then going out into that neighborhood to do what God says. Church involvement. Community service. Neighborhood outreach. Hours and hours of voluntary hard work.

Do not forget that these young people are eager to grow and to learn, as well as to serve. Imagine them discussing good books (they have no television), integrating their faith with real-life issues, learning how to get along with one another under all kinds of pressure, and embracing the values of the kingdom of

God. Not for a week. Not for a month. Imagine them living this way for a whole year.

Can you see what happens? That houseful of people makes a difference in that neighborhood, and, in return, the neighborhood makes a difference in their lives. This living gospel, this body of Christ, transforms—or at least uplifts—everything and everyone it touches. The kingdom of God advances.

Now, finally, imagine all of that ten thousand times over, and you have the vision of Mission Year.

We are not there yet. We are not even close. But I see glimpses of it, and so can everybody else who works with me. The hundreds of young people who have experienced Mission Year over the years can glimpse it too, and so can hundreds more who are already planning to join us in the years to come. It is a great vision, and in every inner-city neighborhood in which we have worked so far, it has been a great reality. That is why all of us are so willing to strive and sacrifice to make it happen.

We need help, of course. Our teams live simply, but they still must have food, shelter, and health insurance. Those young missionaries raise some financial support each year, but not nearly enough to cover their costs. It is an honor for me to spread the news of what God is doing in and through this ministry, but sometimes I struggle to come right out and ask for money. Maybe I should stop trying. Maybe I should just ask people to use their imaginations instead.

THREE

Reading Class

Doris will never learn to read, but she comes to the adult literacy program at the Rock of Our Salvation Church just the same, and only partly because she has to in order to keep her welfare checks coming. Mainly she comes because that adult literacy program is the one place in her life where she knows she will be loved no matter what she can or cannot do, and no matter how often she fails. And fail she does, over and over again, in practically every way imaginable. If you believe that there are born losers in this life, then Doris must surely be among them.

From a purely human perspective, she has practically nothing going for her. For starters, she is mentally handicapped, though not severely enough to qualify for any special benefits. Instead, since very early in her life, she has been left to fend for herself in that especially difficult and dangerous environment known as inner-city Chicago. Somehow she has lived there for nearly fifty years, but those years have more than taken their toll. There were men, too many of them, and never a good one, but now Doris is all alone. Four of her five children are in prison, and the fifth is not much better off.

Poor, illiterate, and practically unemployable, even now Doris' life remains an utterly chaotic and endless succession of conflicts and crises, without purpose or direction. One reason is that, on top of everything else, Doris has become an incredibly difficult person to deal with. At least it seems that way to her teachers at the adult literacy program, and especially to Tommy, a Mission Year team member who has been Doris' primary tutor.

For the better part of the year, Doris wore Tommy out with her disruptive behavior in the classroom. She would speak loudly and out of turn. She would swear and fight with other students and frequently ignore Tommy's instructions altogether. Teaching adult literacy to a class of ten would be difficult under any circumstances (one-on-one is ideal), but with Doris around, it often became absolutely impossible. Yet Tommy kept on trying, day after day, week after week, knowing that, despite her inability to be consistent in any other way, Doris would always be right there waiting for him.

Because she loomed so large in his daily life, Tommy often prayed about Doris, or, more accurately, he prayed about his attitude toward her. Here is what he prayed: "Doris is stupid. Doris is crude. Doris is mean. God, please help me not to hate her."

Certainly this is not how Tommy expected to pray when he first joined Mission Year. He came to love the poor, not to try not to hate them. But with Doris he struggled to control feelings of disgust and despair, feelings he believed a good Christian should not have.

Then one day Doris showed up early, and asked Tommy if he could do her a favor after class. Sure, he replied, wondering what kind of mess she had gotten herself into this time. This was not the first time Doris had asked him for extra help. Usually it had to do with sorting out her bills or with some other convoluted paperwork she could not decipher. Already this year Tommy had spent hours on the phone for Doris, alternately waiting on hold for and arguing with more kinds of caseworkers and agencies than he even knew existed.

After class Tommy sat down across the table from Doris. Quietly she reached into her bag and pulled out an envelope. She handed it to him.

"I got this letter from my oldest son," she said, "but I can't read it. Would you read it for me?"

Tommy opened the envelope and pulled out two crudely lettered pieces of notebook paper. He began to read out loud, but the writing was not easy to understand. Evidently Doris' son was only barely literate himself. Tommy was able to get the gist of the letter, and by adding a few words and repairing some punctuation in his mind, he was able to tell Doris what her son had to say to her. He kept his eyes down and his voice flat. He felt a bit embarrassed to be "overhearing" such a sad and private piece of communication, but there was no help for it.

When he was finished, Doris took back the letter without a word and readied herself to go back out into the world. After a moment of consideration, Tommy ventured a question. "Uh ... Doris? Would you like me to help you write a letter back to him?"

Her face brightened for a moment, and she sat down again. It took them some time to compose Doris' reply, but this time Tommy did not mind. Something supernatural had happened to him. He did not fully recognize it yet, but his prayer had been answered.

"I know it was hard for Doris to ask me to read that letter for her," he explains. "She had been carrying it around with her for a while, I know, but there was nobody in her life whom she felt comfortable enough to show it to. It isn't just that she can't read. It's that her kid's in jail and her life's all messed up, too. All of a sudden, when I was reading that letter, I realized that Doris is who Jesus meant when he talked about the 'poor in spirit,' and I was so glad I was in a position to help her."

There is more.

"Before that night, I never really thought about what I had to offer as a missionary," Tommy continues. "But now I know at least one really powerful way I can help people. I can read! I never thought that was such a big deal, but it is. Now I want to go back to college to learn how to teach reading, but I want to do more than just that. I also want to be the literate, competent, understanding friend who makes life more bearable for people like Doris, people who never had a chance."

No, Doris will never read. But Tommy will. She may be a born loser, but he is a made lover, and Doris is the one God used to make him so. She may be poor in spirit, but Tommy is far richer for having known her. The ironic thing is that Doris thinks Tommy did her a favor.

Perhaps that is the reason Jesus said the kingdom of God is for her.

FOUR

Marcus' Eyes

I spent most of the night on the roof of a row house in North Philadelphia, trying not to let the sounds of nearby chaos spoil the million-dollar view of the skyscrapers in the distance. I was up there talking with the missionaries from our Calvary Church team, one after another, about subjects ranging from day-camp discipline to marriage to existential theology.

The sheer intensity of our program often flushes out deep, vital conflicts and questions in the lives of our volunteers. The culture shock of poverty, the close living conditions, and especially the constant contact with attention-starved, inner-city kids have a way of breaking through all kinds of superficiality. As focused as we are on serving inner-city neighborhoods, I sometimes think our main ministry is helping all these bright, young Christians who through their mission experience work out their discipleship in the storm of some very harsh realities. When it works, those missionaries end up giving God much more than the year they bargained for. For this Calvary team, it seemed to be working overtime, which meant that I had to work overtime as well.

I heard lots of stories on the roof that night, but one told by the team leader hit me harder than the rest.

A few days earlier, Lee told me, their team had thrown a small dinner party at the church for a little boy they knew from their day camp. It was nothing special, really, except for the fact that it was the first time nine-year-old Marcus did not have to compete with anyone else for his counselors' attention. He was thrilled. The team all knew his home situation was miserable, and they had watched him getting pushed around by the other kids at camp, which is why they had invited him over in the first place. If ever there was a kid who needed some tender loving care, it was Marcus.

The team took turns asking Marcus questions, and listened carefully to every word of his answers. He positively bloomed in the spotlight. After dinner they let him help clear the table and do the dishes before breaking out the ice cream and Uno cards. All evening long, Lee said, Marcus' eyes were wide and bright. It was, to him, a rare occasion to be celebrated as special and valuable, and to be cherished as a child, and he loved every minute of it.

"I'll never forget those eyes," Lee said, "especially because of what happened to Marcus later on that night."

After taking Marcus home, Lee said, the team was relaxing back at their own house when they heard the sounds of a fist fight in the back alley. Before long it was clear to them that someone out there was being beaten up. As Lee described the incident, I knew how helpless he and his teammates must have felt. There was nothing they could do. Our safety rules do not allow team members outside after dark and expressly forbid them from trying to intervene in street fights. As any police officer will tell you, there is nothing more dangerous than a stranger trying to break up an altercation between people who know each other. Moreover, it is awfully difficult to figure out who is who or what is going on in the first place, and being wrong about either can get you or somebody else killed.

The beating did not last long. It was over before they could even call the police. I did not tell Lee that I doubt such a call would have made much of a difference anyway. In the neighborhood of Calvary Church, response time is measured in hours, not minutes.

It was Marcus being beaten up in the alley that night. I do not know why he came back out, or how or why it happened. Maybe there was no reason. Lee did not say. Lee did not say much about the beating at all, actually, as I recall. What was there to say about it, except that it is a shame that this world could not leave that little boy alone even for one whole night to let him savor the feeling of being the special one, safe and secure from all alarms?

All Lee told me was that the beating happened, and that it made Marcus' joy at the party all that much more precious to him, and Marcus' eyes all that much more impossible to forget. For the sake of the kingdom, I hope so.

FIVE

Three Wonderful Words

Our church in West Philadelphia is fairly ordinary, but I like it. The worship service is not my style, but I enjoy the fact that the congregation is a truly bizarre array of neighborhood people, most of whom seem genuinely excited about following Jesus. Besides, afterwards there are free donuts and lots of older women who make a fuss over my children.

A few years ago I noticed a teenager there named Eddie Wilson, who came to church each week with the Patrick family. Frankly, Eddie was not very hard to notice. At six-foot-three and close to 250 pounds, he towered over everybody else there. Big as he was, though, Eddie seemed like a shy kid. He rarely spoke to anyone after church except for the Patricks, a young African-American couple, with a little girl, involved with the youth ministry. I tried to strike up a conversation with Eddie a few times, but I did not get very far until the summer my wife, Marty, took over the church's daily vacation Bible school.

Not surprisingly, Marty's first command decision was to place me in charge of recruiting volunteers, a not-so-easy task in a church as small as ours. I did my level best, but the week before VBS was to begin, I was still one teacher short and none of the congregation would let me get within ten feet of them or their spouses. Then, while munching my second donut after church,

I spied Eddie quietly moving toward the back door. Poor kid. Before he knew what hit him, I had him signed, sealed, and delivered for two full weeks.

It turned out that Eddie was a natural with children. Each day, Marty told me, he became more and more animated and involved, so that by the end of VBS he was everybody's favorite volunteer. After that, I had an easy time connecting with Eddie. We joked around almost every Sunday. One day I asked him why he had come to our church in the first place.

"You don't know my story, do you, Bart?" he asked me, as if I was hopelessly behind the times. I shook my head no. He smiled slyly. "Well ... if you and Marty take me out to dinner next week, I'd be glad to tell you all about it." And so I got hustled. I did not mind. Eddie's story was worth much more than the price of dinner.

He was born to a crack-addict mother in North Philadelphia. As far as Eddie was concerned, his father could have been anyone. Whoever he was, he was long gone. Eddie and his older sister shared a precarious existence with their mother until one day, when Eddie was six and his sister was nine, their mother went out to buy drugs and never came back.

"We waited in the apartment for a few weeks," he told us, "but when she didn't come back, the landlord told us we had to leave. So then we were homeless."

Listening to him, Marty and I were horrified at the thought of two small children being abandoned to fend for themselves on big-city streets. I asked how long they were out there before somebody took them in, expecting him to say a few days or maybe a week.

"We were homeless for two years," he answered. "For two

years we begged and stole to survive. In the summer we slept outside. We slept a lot of different places in winter. Sometimes my sister had to do things with men. It was really bad."

Finally, the police picked up Eddie and his sister, and eventually it was discovered that they had relatives in West Philadelphia. Arrangements were made for the children to move in with an aunt they had never met. Eddie said things were better then, but not very much. The aunt was willing enough to have them, though there was little affection. Looking back, he admitted that he and his sister were wild and disrespectful, hardened by their time alone on the street. They fought everything, especially school. By the time he was fourteen, Eddie's sister had run off with an older man, and Eddie did little more than deal drugs and play basketball at the local playground. It was there, he said, that he met Mrs. Patrick.

"Everybody at the playground knew Mrs. Patrick," he explained, "because she was short, and she wore dreadlocks ... and she could play basketball better than any dude on the court!" A former Division 1 athletic star, Mrs. Patrick was also a serious trash talker, who delighted in playfully taunting the bigger, younger boys she routinely wiped out one-on-one. After a while, however, she took a special interest in Eddie.

"She used to tell me all the time, 'I see you, Eddie'; 'you're special, Eddie'; 'there's something good about you'; and stuff like that. When she saw me on the corner selling drugs, she'd say, 'How was school today? You should have been there to find out.' Then one day she told me I should come on over to have dinner at their house."

At the Patrick house, Eddie ate a sit-down dinner, with conversation instead of television, for the first time. After the dishes had been cleared, everyone sat on the floor to play with the baby. He loved it. After that, he became a regular. As time went on, Mr. Patrick took him to a few professional ball games. Mrs. Patrick invited him to youth group.

Then one day, back at the playground, Eddie and Mrs. Patrick got into an argument over a called foul, and Eddie said something way out of line. Her reply was perfect. "You still don't get it, do you Eddie? I love you. My husband loves you. And our God loves you too."

Three words broke Eddie's heart wide open.

"When she said, 'I love you,' well, that was it for me. In my whole life no one had ever said those words to me. After that I would have done anything in the world for that woman. I would have killed whoever tried to hurt her. I would have gone anywhere she told me to go, and done anything she told me to do." He paused for a moment, and then he smiled. "Well, she told me to come to church, and she told me to accept Jesus, and that's why I go there and that's why I'm a Christian."

A few years later, Eddie Wilson no longer goes to our church, but not because he went back to dealing drugs. No, Eddie is away at college now. Before he went, though, he was the star of our youth group's mission trip to Mexico.

Simply stated, there is no way that a crack baby left homeless on the streets of North Philadelphia for two years at the age of six should be in college. He should be dead; at the very least, he should be in jail. He should be your worst urban nightmare, a dangerous criminal with no conscience or a junkie in the gutter with no hope. Instead, Eddie Wilson is a disciple of Jesus, because somebody loved him the same way Jesus loves you and me.

Mrs. Patrick picked him out of the crowd. She and her husband made him part of their lives and part of their family. They stuck with him until the time was right, until Mrs. Patrick spoke those three wonderful words that changed his life forever. Those same three words that Jesus speaks to you and me: I love you.

SIX

A Tale of
Two Neighbors

People who rarely venture into the inner city often perceive our young missionaries to be spiritual pioneers, ministering to forgotten people who have seldom if ever been reached by the gospel. In fact, their neighborhoods are practically overrun by Christian evangelists of every style. What distinguishes Mission Year is not our boldness, but rather the fact that we do not hit and run. This is not a high-powered evangelism ministry. There are plenty of those already. This is a settle-down-and-love-your-neighbor ministry, where the evangelism has to come naturally if it comes at all.

Annie up the street, for instance, does not need to be evangelized. Wasting away in her dingy little apartment, a walking skeleton with full-blown AIDS, she already believes in God. She hasn't been to church in years, but Annie is a Christian. Like so many believers, however, she seems awfully confused about God's true nature. One day she says her slow death is punishment for her sins, the next she is sure God will heal and help her. I know this only because her dearest friends as she dies are the women of one of our teams.

Annie is up and down, they tell me, both physically and spiritually, with little left to hope for except the return of her long-lost boyfriend, who apparently abandoned her to deal with his own case of AIDS. Her more recent Mission Year friends, on the other hand, are eager to share her life. They are happy with her when she is happy, complimenting her choice of clothes, and celebrating when she manages to eat a meal. But then they suffer when she suffers, too, and they feel helpless to do more than listen to her talk on and on about her short and difficult life.

Annie is only twenty-eight, but, to hear her tell it, people stopped listening to her a long time ago. She wore them out, I suppose. People who are falling apart have a way of doing that, so that after a while they are falling apart alone. That is why Annie loves these strange new women who have moved in out of nowhere, she tells them. Because they keep coming back to listen, and because when they do, they listen like nobody else in her life.

As they tell me about Annie, I see a quality in these women that was not there when they joined us in September. They may feel helpless, but bearing Annie's burden over these months has made them strong. She will die, of course, as all people die, but she will die in good company, beloved and reassured of God's boundless mercy for his children. Annie was already saved when our women met her, and yet she still needed salvation. I am so glad it found her.

At the other end of the block lives Fatima, who has already embraced not one but two religions. The first time was a decade ago, when Fatima's name was Diane and she was strung out on cocaine. The church folks who came to her then were a godsend, she says, and they helped her first to bury her hatred and later to reclaim her children from foster care. She was grateful, and as her life came together, she became a faithful member of that same church.

Unfortunately, those same church folks, who knew so well what to do with an addict, were not so clear about what to do with an ex-addict. Growing in her faith, Diane eventually began to express interest in joining the ministry teams and committees that signified Christian maturity in her church, only to find that the very people who had rescued her did not trust the authenticity of her transformation enough to give her any real responsibility.

As any drug rehabilitation counselor will attest, for a recovering addict, self-esteem is both essential and fragile. Generally speaking, this is a person who repeatedly has been told that she or he is worthless and incapable of real change. Once a junkie, always a junkie, the saying goes. Sadly, the fear that saying expresses has undone more than a few borderline people who were barely hanging on to recovery.

The distrust of her church did not undo Diane. She did not return to drugs. Instead, she left that church in frustration, married a devout and honorable Muslim man, and became a Muslim herself. I suppose that on a very practical level the good man she married and his community of faith represented a better opportunity for her to start her life over again. She became a devout Muslim, too, which is certainly the main reason it took those same Mission Year women who had befriended Annie so long to get to know her. Dressed from head to toe in her religious garb, this good Muslim woman now known as Fatima must have figured it would be a waste of her time to talk to these new, obviously Christian neighbors.

Eventually, however, Fatima noticed that these aggressively

friendly newcomers were much more interested in playing with her children than in questioning her theology. What began as front-porch greetings led to longer conversations and much later to a cautiously accepted dinner invitation. It was over that dinner that our team finally heard Fatima tell her story.

As they tell me about their relationship with the wonderful Muslims a few weeks later, our missionaries wonder out loud what to do next. What does it mean for them as Christian missionaries to minister to Fatima and her family?

In the team's opinion, straightforward evangelism would not only prove futile, but would also be positively inappropriate. These Muslims plainly came into their neighbors' Christian home under the banner of friendship, after all, and trusted them enough to be open about their journey of faith. What's more, Fatima and her family are not nominal Muslims but devoted believers whose religion gives meaning and order to their daily lives and relationships. They bear the fruit of the Spirit. To outward appearances, they are in touch with God already.

And yet our missionaries are uncomfortable. As evangelical Christians, they feel wrong leaving well enough alone, unless that "well enough" involves an evangelical Christian guarantee of salvation. In their minds, to accept their Muslim friends without trying to reconvert them is to consign those friends to everlasting and irrevocable damnation. This, of course, they are unwilling to do.

What our team works out together in the end is perfectly simple and, I think, simply perfect: They resolve not to try to convince Fatima and her family to abandon Islam or return to formal Christianity. In fact, they resolve not to talk with her at all about comparative religion or theology. Instead, they decide to talk with her about Jesus himself and Jesus alone.

After all, they reason, as a Muslim, Fatima is bound to admire and respect Jesus. Indeed, regardless of religion, people the world over respect Jesus, if not as their Savior then as a prophet or at least as a great moral teacher. They may hate Christianity. They may fear evangelical Christians. But practically everybody seems to love Jesus.

Of course, most of those people who claim to admire, respect, and even love Jesus, including most Christians, are woefully unfamiliar with his life and teachings, as recorded in the four Gospels and the Book of Acts. As a result, most of those people, including most Christians, fail to truly follow after him regardless of what they believe.

So, our team decides, why not start there? Why not just do for their Muslim friends the same thing they were trying to do for Annie and their other neighbors and for one another, as well: encourage them to follow the life and the teachings of Jesus of Nazareth? That way there would be no cause to argue, no reason to discredit anyone else's religion. Instead there would be common ground, a place to begin talking about those things that matter most. Let Jesus speak for himself, they decide, and trust that he is indeed the Way, the Truth, and the Life.

It all sounds quite natural as they explain it to me. But then I wonder, *Is that really evangelism?* Call it what you will. For myself, I put it in the same category as helping Annie die in good company. Against such things, there is no law.

SEVEN

An Unlikely Rescue

She was lost even before she got off the bus. Looking out the windows at the unfamiliar street signs, she realized while studying her directions she had missed her stop. Pulling the bell cord to notify the driver, she stood and made her way to the door, figuring it was a simple enough matter to cross over and wait for the next bus going in the opposite direction. She should have looked around more carefully and waited for a better corner, but she did not know that at the time. She was new to the city, after all.

Sometimes in the midafternoon you have to wait a long time for the next bus. It can seem even longer when you are the only college girl on the street in a bad part of town. At first she had mainly been worried about being late to her appointment at the community center where she hoped to volunteer, but standing out there at that bus stop, all by herself in the hot sun, she began to worry about her safety.

Behind her on the corner was a small grocery store, the kind you see in every inner-city neighborhood, with a liquor store beside it. Beyond the liquor store, slumped in the doorway of a shabby old apartment building, sat a shabby old man with a telltale brown paper bag in one hand. In many ways this neighborhood looked just like the neighborhood a few miles away, where the young woman and her missionary teammates were living and working and going to church, except over here nobody knew her, and she was all by herself.

A group of young men came out of the grocery store, talking loud and laughing. As soon as they noticed her, she knew she was in trouble. They called to her. "Hey girl, whatchoo doin' around here?" "Ooh, you lookin' good, sister!" "How about a date?" They were smiling, but their voices were edged with menace.

She just stood there staring straight ahead as she had been trained to do, knowing that there was no good way to respond, hoping the young men would give up and leave her alone. Instead, they moved in closer, surrounding her, and taunted her for ignoring them. "What's the problem, girl? You think you're too good for us? We'll see about that." Egging one another on, they began describing the awful things they were going to do to her.

She looked around in every direction, desperate for someone who might help her, but there was no help in sight. Silent and terrified, she prayed to God.

Suddenly, into the circle of young men stumbled the old wino had been sitting in the doorway down the street. "Wait just a minute!" he said in a loud voice, "What's going on here?" He looked directly at the young woman. "Tell me your name."

Without thinking, she told him. The young men did not interrupt.

"Where do you live?" he asked her, and again she answered. Then he asked her age and then a few more questions, until he seemed satisfied that he had enough information. Finally, he turned to face the first of her tormentors.

"You know that you should not be doing this to her, don't you?" he demanded. He moved in front of the next young man in the circle. "And you! You know you should not be doing this, either." One by one he confronted them, while the frightened missionary looked on in amazement. When he was finished, they were gone.

The old man paused for a moment, and then walked back toward his doorway. The relieved young woman reached out to stop him, to thank him, but he pulled away from her. He looked at her for a moment, but without registering even a glimmer of recognition. His eyes were vacant again, as they had been when she saw him before. The ruffians had left, and it seemed to her that the brave old man who had come out to save her was gone as well, lost in the depths of his own weary soul.

And so the young missionary was rescued, by God and by one of God's prodigal sons. Another bus came by, finally, and she found her way back home, safe and sound. And so, we may hope, will the prodigal son who saved her.

EIGHT

What's Your Job?

What's your job?"

The question surprised me. There we were, four teenaged boys and I all wedged into a booth at Burger King, each with his Bible in one hand and his Whopper in the other. We came here every Thursday afternoon, for a small-group discipleship meeting unapologetically founded on my pastor's ability to come up with free meal coupons from the Burger King corporation. I had been close to most of these boys for two or three years, but lately we had added a new member to the group, and he was full of new questions. This one, however, seemed to have nothing to do with the Scripture passage we were studying. I suggested that we try to stay focused.

"No, I'm serious, Bart. What's your job? What do you do for a living?"

Impatiently, I explained to my young friend that what I did for a living was what I was doing right then, that my job was working with neighborhood kids. I run youth group meetings, I pointed out to him. I come out to your ball games and concerts. I take you guys on camping trips and weekend retreats and talk with you about your relationships with God. The more I described my job to this newcomer, the more confused he seemed to become.

"Who pays you to do this job?"

I work for a nonprofit ministry organization, I explained. Wealthy people from the suburbs contribute money each month, which our organization gathers together and packages up for me as a paycheck, so that I can live in the city and hang out with you guys.

Still, he looked puzzled. Then, all of a sudden, a look of recognition passed across his face. "Oh, I get it," he said confidently, with not even a hint of irony in his voice. "You're on welfare." The other boys laughed, but he earnestly continued. "It's Christian welfare, I guess, but it sounds pretty much the same. You're getting paid just to hang out. That's cool, I guess."

But all of a sudden it was not cool with me. In that instant I realized for the first time that I was no role model for these inner-city kids I loved so much. There I was preaching that they had to learn how to work for a living, that with the help of God they had to stand on their own two feet, while all the time I was the most dependent person in the neighborhood. I was the one living off rich people. I was the one sending out letters every month begging for more money.

None of these kids could ever be like me, unless by some miracle he was suddenly transformed into a white upper-middle-class college graduate with a Christian family and friends willing and able to support his ministry habits. None of them was a child of privilege. But I was. I am.

At the same time, I also realized that these guys sitting with me at the Burger King were looking at me in a new way. Up until then, they had not given much thought to the economics of our relationship. Once they did, they did not much like their conclusions. Before, they had assumed that I hung out with them simply because I cared about them. Now they realized that it was my job. I was a professional youth worker. In other words, I was paid to be their friend. And that changed everything.

I did my best to salvage things. I insisted to them that there was no way I was in this for the money. With my education and connections, I pointed out, I could be making a whole lot more doing something else. I was living and working with them in the inner city because I loved them, plain and simple. And, for their information, there was a lot more to it than just hanging out. Whether or not I convinced them, however, was beside the point. (I knew better myself.) I had lost faith in myself.

Try as I might, the role models those kids really needed were not like me at all. What they needed were men and women who had grown up where they were growing up, and who had faced all the trials and tribulations that they were facing now, and who had overcome it all to become strong and healthy and good. What they needed were Christian adults from the neighborhood, with real lives and real jobs, who they knew ran youth groups and hung out with them only because they cared. Black, Hispanic, Asian, white inner-city people, with families to share, values to teach, and a passionate love for God. What they needed were inner-city church folks.

Do not get me wrong. I did not pack up and go home the day after my enlightenment at the Burger King. As a matter of fact, I did not pack up and go home at all. For one thing, I figured that even a non-role model like myself was better than nothing for the kids with whom I was working. Local heroes, unfortunately, are always in short supply. Besides that, I figured that even if inner-city church volunteers were the best kind of inner-city youth workers, there was still an important role for the professional in setting up programs to make those folks more effective in the limited amount of time they had to give. My mind was changed that day, however, and it has stayed changed.

Sure, Mission Year brings into the city lots of white, upper-middle-class college graduates whose bills are paid by Christian families and friends willing and able to support their ministry habits. We believe that they have something to contribute here, as well as something to learn. Outside missionaries, however, are not the people who will save the city. No, the people who will save the city are and must be the people who, by the grace of God, already live there.

NINE

Pick-Up Hoops

With his mouth the godless destroys his neighbor,
but through knowledge the righteous escape.

PROVERBS 11:9

During the summer months I play pick-up basketball at two very different parks. Narberth, in the nicest of suburbs, is a beautifully landscaped place, with two pristine courts right next to a tree-shaded playground. I usually play there on weekends, while my children run around having their own kind of fun.

Parkside, in a rough part of the city, is definitely no place for kids. The concrete courts are usually clear, but the grass around them is strewn with garbage and broken glass, and all the playground equipment is busted. I only go there late on week nights, after my children are safely tucked in their beds. It may sound dangerous, but basketball players are generally not much trouble, and at Parkside there are always lots of ball games running until well after midnight.

Being the only white man on the court, I always get into the games at Parkside right away, either because everyone is afraid to look prejudiced or because everyone is curious to see how I play. At Narberth, on the other hand, I often have to wait, because the locals there tend to favor their own. And nobody calls me Larry Bird.

A few years go I nearly got into big trouble on a Saturday morning at Narberth. The game started out innocently, but soon enough the play got physical. Nobody said anything about it, however, until I jumped up high and blocked from behind the shot of a player on the other team. Before I knew what was happening, this fellow spun around and pushed me to the ground with both hands, cursing me loudly at the same time. I was stunned for a moment, as was everyone else on both teams, but I quickly scrambled back to my feet.

Unfortunately, while doing so I verbalized my displeasure in a distinctly unspiritual manner, which as it happened was not a very good idea. By the way, did I mention yet that this player who knocked me down was roughly six-foot-three, weighed at least 250 pounds, and was built like Arnold Schwarzenegger?

He stepped right up to me, jabbing his index finger into my chest. His reply was unquotable, but it boiled down to "Shut your mouth, jerk, before I really mess you up. You wanna fight right now? No, I didn't think so." He paused and then leaned over until his face was close to mine. "You better watch yourself, or you're gonna get hurt. You need to pump some iron, you little punk. I can do whatever I want to you, and there's nothing you can do about it."

I did indeed shut my mouth, but my foolish pride kept me from walking away. Instead, I tried to outplay the big guy and stay out of his way at the same time, failing miserably on both counts. He was not much of a basketball player, but after his outburst nobody was even trying to stop him when he drove to the hoop. Certainly I was not going to challenge him one-on-one. He kept scoring baskets, each time stopping to taunt me afterward. I did my best to hold my own, but my confidence was shattered. Besides, the big guy kept banging me around, whether or not I had the ball, daring me to do something about it. He never stopped talking trash until the game was over. When it finally ended, and I began to walk off the court, he stepped in front of me and laughed in my face.

I wish I could say I shrugged it off, but the truth is that I was absolutely furious at being so humiliated. For the first time in a long time, I had been made to feel weak and small. The more I thought about it, the more enraged I became. Frightening as it sounds, all I could think of was revenge. I wanted to walk up to that bully and shove a gun in his face. "You think you're so tough?" I wanted to scream, "You think you're so funny? Well, laugh at this, tough guy!" In that moment, I wanted to see the same helpless fear in his eyes that he had seen in mine.

Weird, huh? There I was, a secure, educated man with a loving family, a fine career, and a deep faith in God, sitting in my car in a playground parking lot fantasizing about violence. As soon as I caught myself, this thought hit me like a bullet: *What if I did not have all of those things? What if I were insecure and uneducated, alone and without a job? What if I had no faith at all? What if I were just another dead-end kid in the city, feeling as if everyone and everything kept pushing me around and putting me down?*

And then, what if I had a gun?

Pleasant words are a honeycomb,
sweet to the soul and healing to the bones.

PROVERBS 16:24

A few nights later I drove over to Parkside. It was late and hot, but nobody seemed to notice. The park was full of basketball players, but the only-white-guy thing worked as usual, and I got on the court right away. Better still, I got on a good team, which meant we stayed out there for nearly three hours, taking on all comers. Normally I do not play so long, but this time I felt too good to leave. Honestly, I cannot remember the last time I had so much fun.

It was not just the winning that energized me, though certainly winning beats losing every time. It was not that I played especially well, either, though I certainly played better than I had the other day at Narberth. No, what made this particular night so great was this very special big guy named Terry. Somehow, he lit up everybody's night.

For the sake of the uninitiated, let me simply explain that inner-city pick-up basketball games are seldom settings in which one experiences moments of great humanity. There is generally no profound dialogue or meaningful interaction. Basketball players banter back and forth with one another, of course, and often curse and shout and argue. Until I played with Terry, however, I never saw a basketball player who could sing, philosophize, make jokes, break up fights, encourage teammates, commend opponents, offer advice, and thoroughly entertain onlookers—while all the time dominating the game. I have seen my share of great players before and since, but this guy was something special. Terry was a one-man party that night, and it seemed as if everybody in the park was invited.

He had the players on our team introduce ourselves to one another before our first game started, but soon he had given each one of us some kind of goofy nickname. He might not have gotten away with that except that he was clearly the best player on either side. Still, he did not hog the ball or show off very much. His best moves usually ended up with passes to wide-open teammates instead of shots. He took over on offense only a few times all night, always late in the game when our team was in danger of losing. When he did, his shooting was deadly accurate.

So was his sense of humor. Clever as he was, I knew that a guy like Terry could get into trouble out there awfully fast, but he seemed to instinctually know just how far he could go with people. Besides, like his basketball game, Terry's joking around was calculated to make everyone look good and get everyone involved.

At one point, between games, Terry pulled a video camera out of his battered old car, happily running around the park like some lunatic sportscaster, "interviewing" people and making them laugh. These were not little kids he was fooling around with, either, but grown men in a hard place. Yet somehow he made everything and everybody work together for good.

Even as I write about him, I am afraid that much of Terry's charm gets lost in the translation. I suppose this is one of those experiences of which it must be said you really had to be there. Out of nowhere one night, for the sheer joy of it, this big guy named Terry made a bunch of strangers in an inner-city park into friends, and in doing so ministered to me in an unbelievable way.

It went on like that until two in the morning, when the lights in the park shut off and left us there in the dark. There was nothing to do but go home. Like a star-struck little boy, I hurried over to shake Terry's hand before he got into his car and asked him when he might be back again. "Oh, you never know where I'm gonna show up next," he said with a mischievous grin, "because I never know myself. But whenever it is, I'll be glad to see you." And with that he was gone.

Right away I missed him. It may seem foolish, but I found myself repeating in my mind his kind words to me, strangely warmed by the affirmation of someone I genuinely admired. That, I told myself, is the kind of person I want to be.

Weird, huh? There I was, a secure, educated man with a loving family, a fine career, and a deep faith in God, sitting in my car in a playground parking lot hero-worshiping a most-likely unemployed inner-city pick-up basketball player. As soon as I caught myself, this thought hit me like a ray of light: What a difference from that terrible day at Narberth! What a difference one person can make in this world, if that person is armed with true love!

And then, what if Terry had been the one that other big guy had pushed down?

TEN

A Lesson in Badness

First, a little urban language seminar. In the inner city, "bad" is good. Therefore the phrase *That jacket is bad,* when spoken by someone around here, can be loosely translated, *That is a very nice jacket.* Actually, bad means a lot more than very nice. Bad means strong and cool and even a bit dangerous sometimes. Bad is an attitude. A rap musician can be bad, for example. A basketball player like Shaquille O'Neal is super bad.

I am not bad at all. Never have been. Probably never will be. After more than twenty years of living and working with some of the world's baddest individuals, I still have one of the world's lowest badness quotients around. I have not survived here in the city by intimidating anybody, but rather by having enough sense to avoid trouble most of the time and enough wit to talk myself out of trouble the rest of the time. In other words, I am streetwise.

When I first came to the city, however, I was the exact opposite of streetwise. Having grown up on a small college campus in a main-line suburb of Philadelphia, I knew practically nothing about how to get by in the harsh urban environment popularly known as the ghetto. During that first summer, my inexperience was not too much of a problem, mainly because I was only a day-camp counselor for little kids. I stayed safely tucked away in the basement of a church during the daytime and drove back out to my home in the suburbs at night. The next year, however, I actually moved into the city, to work on the streets and playgrounds of a really run-down, low-cost housing project.

As soon as I got there, I knew I was in trouble. I was supposed to be in charge of the day camp this time, but none of the kids seemed to know it. Outside, in front of the entire community, those kids made a fool out of me. They talked out of turn. They pushed. They fought. Nobody listened or followed directions. By the time they went home after lunch, I was completely defeated. I was also scared. All morning long I had watched hostile-looking teenagers and adults walking by the day camp, staring at me and the other suburbanite counselors with disapproval. The whole situation seemed dangerous.

A skinny teenager approached me. "Yo, man, you're not from around here, are you?" he asked.

I smiled weakly. "How could you tell?" He laughed at the joke.

"Look, man, I've been watching you. You better know you ain't gonna last very long in here with that lame act you runnin'. You need help. How 'bout I show you around here a little bit, you know, so you don't go gettin' killed just trying to run some little ole day camp?"

I may not be bad, but I definitely am not suicidal. I knew better than to turn down an offer like that. The kid's name was Tyrone. He was only fourteen years old, but that summer he saved my life.

Day after day he walked me around the project after camp,

introducing me to people, telling me where I could and could not go, and who I could and could not talk to. From Tyrone I learned to understand what people were saying to me, and what they meant. He could not make me instantly streetwise, of course, but he made sure I stayed out of major trouble. In return, I told him about Jesus. By summer's end, two good things were true: I was still alive. And Tyrone was a Christian.

Tyrone was also my friend. As I soon discovered, this was no ordinary kid. Blessed with a good mind, a quick tongue, and a handsome face, Tyrone appeared to everyone as supremely self-confident. He was funny, too. It did not surprise me when I discovered that he was particularly popular among the teenaged girls who were always hanging around the playground. It also did not surprise me that the other day-camp counselors were a little bit jealous of our relationship. After all, working so closely with a kid like Tyrone is every urban missionary's dream.

Then one evening toward the end of the summer, Tyrone appeared at the door of the missionary house with a strange look on his face. "Yo, Bart," he said, "my mom threw me out of my apartment. I got nowhere else to go. I gotta come live with you now."

At first I was not worried. Kids were always coming by our place asking to live with us, and for good reason. In contrast to their dimly lit and often crowded apartments, our house was clean and bright, with plenty of room and lots of food in the refrigerator. Besides, what kid would not want to live in a house full of friendly adults who consider it their jobs to play all day long? When kids said they had been thrown out, we would say, "Fine, let's go ask your mom about that," knowing that halfway home the story would suddenly change from thrown out to sent out for a quart of milk or some such thing. Tyrone, however, did not change his story. As a matter of fact, Tyrone never said a word while we were walking back over to his apartment.

When we got there, I heard loud voices behind the door. When it opened, there was Tyrone's mother, whom I had met a few times before. Looking at her son now, her face was filled with contempt. She turned to me. "You get that piece of garbage out of my face," she said. "I never want to see him again." Then she slammed the door shut, and Tyrone and I walked back out onto the street.

I asked him what was going on. What had he done? Why was his mother throwing him out? By now he was crying, but eventually the story came out.

"She's throwing me out 'cause I won't bust up the kid who lives across the hall from us. We just found out that boy's been raping my little brother, so now she wants me to hurt him bad so he don't do it no more. But I told her Bart says that Jesus says you can't be hurting other people like that, so she threw me out."

I was stunned. I knew Tyrone's brother. He was in our day camp, though he had barely smiled or said a word since it started. Now I understood his silence. He was traumatized by abuse. I told Tyrone we needed to call the police.

"Come on, Bart! You been 'round here long enough to know better than that."

In the projects, I was learning, things worked differently. While I had been raised to trust police officers and the justice system, Tyrone had been raised to fear them for good reason. My privilege guaranteed that I would be treated with fairness and respect, but he knew better than to expect the same. He was always showing me ways the system was broken here. In this case, the boy's tormentor was a convicted criminal already, but still allowed home on weekends from some halfway house. It fell to Tyrone's mother to protect her little boy. Now I understood her anger, too.

"You tell me what to do," he said.

I had no good answer, and both of us knew it. There was no good answer. All summer long I had been teaching Tyrone and the kids in the day camp about Christian nonviolence. I believe in Christian nonviolence. In the city, of all places, you learn very fast that one beating only leads to another, that violence does not solve a problem so much as it displaces it for a time. It is wrong to send a kid out to bust up another kid. Then again, it is also wrong to let somebody rape your little brother.

"Go find that boy, Tyrone," I said. "You go find him, and you hurt him. Hurt him so bad that he never comes near your brother again, do you hear?"

And then I went back to my clean, bright house, with plenty of room and lots of food in the refrigerator, and I got down on my knees and asked God to forgive me.

When I got up again, I felt different. I felt dirty, in a way, just being involved with such terrible things, but more than that I felt fallen. In that awful moment I realized for the first time that out there in the real world the choices are not always between right and wrong, but sometimes between bad and worse. My cut-and-dried Sunday school answers had worked fine for me growing up as a child of privilege in the suburbs, but for kids like Tyrone and his brother, and for women like their mother, a certain amount of violence was and is a matter of survival. I might or might not choose to be good. They had to be "bad."

I would not dare to suggest a singular definition of the kingdom of God, but I am certain of this much: A child will grow up there without ever having to sin to save his brother.

ELEVEN

Who Needs More?

I often make people uncomfortable when I talk about inner-city kids. I tell stories about their lives and their struggles, about their poverty and the terrible consequences it brings down on them. I get emotional when I describe the way I know that God grieves for his little ones who suffer. People tell me I make it seem as though somehow God loves the poor people and kids in trouble more than he loves the rest of us, as though they are actually closer to his heart and more on his mind. When they tell me this, I struggle to respond.

But recently a friend showed me a passage from Mark's Gospel that I found curiously helpful. In this passage Mary Magdalene, the other Mary, and Salome have gone to anoint Jesus' body. When they reach the tomb, the stone blocking the entrance has already been rolled away. Inside, they are met by an angel.

> *"Don't be alarmed," he said. "You are looking for Jesus the Nazarene, who was crucified. He has risen! He is not here. See the place where they laid him. But go, tell his disciples and Peter, 'He is going ahead of you into Galilee. There you will see him, just as he told you.'"*
>
> MARK 16:6-7

What is odd, my friend pointed out, is the special reference to Peter. In this miraculously triumphant moment, why does God's angel pause to single him out? Was not Peter a disciple just like James, John, and the rest of them? All of them had left behind their former lives to follow Jesus, and all of them had lost everything when he was crucified. Now all of them were in hiding, in fear of the same authorities who had killed their leader. Was there something special about Peter that made him different from the others?

The answer, I think, is yes and no. Certainly all of the disciples needed to hear the good news about Jesus' resurrection, which gave them hope for a new life. But Peter, the disciple who had denied Jesus three times, needed something more than good news.

Remember, this was the same man who had boasted to Jesus that he would stand firm even if all the others fell away, who had insisted that he would die with Jesus rather than disown him. But then, when everything had turned against him, Peter had turned as well. Three times he lied to save his own skin. And after the third time, the rooster had crowed twice, just as Jesus had said it would, so that Peter knew that Jesus knew he had sold him out after all.

All of the disciples needed to know Jesus was risen from the dead, but I believe Peter needed to know something more: that the Jesus who was alive again still loved him enough to take him back in spite of his failure. Peter needed the gospel and then some. So Jesus gave him that "and then some," by leaving word that all the disciples—but most especially Peter—were to meet him in Galilee.

Imagine what it must have felt like to Peter when he heard

from those women what the angel had said. He was still in! He was still a disciple! Jesus knew everything that had happened. But still, in the midst of the greatest of triumphs of all time, he had still had the presence of mind to leave a special message just for Peter, to let him know he was wanted in Galilee.

So then, did Jesus love Peter more than the others?

Of course he did, because he knew that at that moment Peter needed more of his love. And does Jesus love our inner-city kids more, as well? Of course he does, for exactly the same reason. Because, without question, those kids need more of his love.

Remember that God's love for us is not just a matter of good feelings; God's love is good action, too. It is food for the hungry and shelter for the vulnerable and healing for the sick. It is a chance to learn how to read and write and work, and a second chance if you blew it the first time. It is having more than enough people who care for you at all times, whether you deserve it or not. It is providence. Some people need more of that good action at this moment, because they have had less up till now. So then God must love those people more, or at least God must want to love them more.

Which, I think, is where you and I come in. Like that angel Jesus left at the empty tomb with a special message for Peter, we too are God's servants in this world, left here to give people the gospel and then some. If we are willing, God wants to use us to love his people from wherever they are to that great and glorious place where he wants them to be, where he wants all of us to be. Some people, like the troubled kids I talk and write about, need a bit more of a special kind of love—the good-action kind—to get there, which is why we still have to have ministries like Mission Year in this world.

Please do not misunderstand me. All of this does not mean God loves the rest of us any less. It just means that God always knows where we are coming from, and exactly what we need.

TWELVE

Cookout on Simpson Street

Our young missionaries hit the home stretch sometime in July. At that point, after almost ten full months in their neighborhoods, they are awfully tired of working so hard, and yet strangely energized by what God has done and is doing through them. In many ways, it is their very best time of ministry. They know their way around, and they know the people around them. The kids are out of school, and the heat has everyone out of doors, so there are even more opportunities than usual for our young missionaries to show their love and share their faith.

A handful of them had a cookout one July Saturday on Simpson Street, which police call one of the worst streets in Philadelphia. You might call it that, too, unless you were sitting on our team's front porch that day, watching their neighbors come and go. To be sure, those neighbors included not a few drug dealers and addicts, beggars, thieves, and just plain down-and-out people hanging onto the edge of society. But at this particular cookout, everybody was welcome, and there was food enough to go around. More than enough, really, because hardly any of the church folks the team invited decided to come.

In that way, this particular cookout was a lot like the great banquet Jesus describes in Luke 14. There, the story goes, the invited guests made excuse after excuse for not coming, until finally the master ordered his servant, "Go out quickly into the streets and alleys of the town and bring in the poor, the crippled, the blind and the lame" (v. 21). Here, on the other hand, everybody was invited in the first place. In both cases, however, only the outcasts showed up.

There was Sharice, who lived in a filthy, unsafe house and routinely endured the jeers of kids amused by her disabilities. And the Jackson boys, who would fight anyone, anytime, with or without provocation, stayed at the cookout for hours and stayed in peace. Mrs. Wilson could not eat the food, but she came anyway, just to socialize. Some Muslim friends came as well, secure that here were Christians who would be happy to have them. People like that were there all evening, happy to be together at the home of those crazy outsiders who moved in last September to make friends. In a weird way, it all seemed quite natural.

Unfortunately, it also seemed quite natural to both the missionaries and their guests that there were hardly any church folks there, and that what few showed up left in a hurry. Do not get me wrong. Most of the time Mission Year is very good at choosing the right churches to work with, that is, churches that are already deeply involved in reaching out to those who are hurting in their neighborhoods. Once in a while, though, we don't make a good match, and the team ends up reaching out on its own, which invariably means that most of the good they do ends abruptly when they leave in August, because the church doesn't continue a hands-on follow-up ministry. This team on Simpson Street, for instance, knew better than to think anyone at their church was going to come out to eat with ghetto rejects.

Why is that? Why do so many of us Christians have such a hard time hanging around the very people whom Jesus most enjoyed when he was here with us?

A quiet voice tells me to look in the mirror, and, sure enough, I find answers to that question. Outcasts make me uncomfortable. I am always too busy either judging or trying to "fix" messed-up people to ever relax and enjoy them. I am always too busy, period. What's more, being with poor people makes me feel selfish and guilty. I want to protect my family. I get scared.

Like most people, including most church people, I have my reasons. When I write them down, though, those reasons do not seem good enough.

Maybe I should ponder again the final line of Jesus' story, where the master declares that once his house is full of outcasts, no one who made excuses gets even a taste of his great feast.

Better still, maybe I should just go ahead and have a cookout, like the one they had on Simpson Street.

THIRTEEN

The Hard Truth

People love statistics. Everywhere you look in this country, somebody is quantifying something. Economic growth. Per capita spending. America's Top Forty. The batting average of left-handed shortstops named Cedric between 1950 and 1975. The list goes on and on, and somewhere on the Internet I bet that somebody has already calculated exactly how long that list will be by Y3K.

Of course, Christian people are no different from anyone else in this respect, particularly when it comes to our ministerial endeavors. When it comes to saving souls, we want to know just how many heathen showed up at the meeting, and just how many came forward and signed on the dotted line, so to speak. I know that better than most people, because as an urban missionary I have to make up all kinds of statistics every year, to justify my annual budget.

Do not get me wrong. When I say I make up statistics, I do not mean that I lie. On the contrary, it is a point of pride with me that I never give out a number for anything that happens in my ministry that is not absolutely accurate and verifiable. What I make up are not my numbers, but rather the abstract categories they measure. Number of significant relational contacts per week. Hours per month spent in evangelism and pre-evangelism. Approximate dollar value of community service work per team per year. Let me tell you, religious foundations and church missions committees eat that stuff up.

Of course, the big statistic for most of us evangelical Christians is conversions, plain and simple. When it comes time to measure the value of our ministries, the first number we look at is how many bona fide converts they produce. In terms of fund-raising, that is unfortunate for me, because Christian converts are the one thing I believe I must refuse to count, especially here in the city.

I did not always feel this way. When I first started out in this work, I used to take great pride in the number of conversions we had each year, which far exceeded anything I had ever seen growing up in the suburbs. But, over time, as I watched kid after kid come forward to give their lives to God, only to drift right back into street life a few weeks or months later, I became disillusioned.

The first kid I can remember losing, the one who started the change in my thinking, was Howard, whom I met during my second summer in the city. He was the leader of a small local street gang in the housing project where I was working, and he and his friends used to love to hang around the playground and disrupt our day camp. As the weeks went by, it got worse and worse. Finally, scared though I was, I had no choice but to confront them.

"Hey, you guys," I said, walking over to the fence they were leaning on. "Why do you want to make things so hard for us? Can't you see that we're just trying to do something good for all these little kids?"

Howard stepped forward, six-foot-two and built like a tank. "So what about us, Mister Super Christian?" he asked. "Why don't y'all try to do something good for us? We ain't got nothing goin' on." The other boys nodded in agreement.

I was still in college back then, not much older than Howard and his gang, but I sensed they thought I was older and had something to offer them, and I was not prone to tell them otherwise. Instead, I found myself promising to start an evening youth group, if only they would leave my day camp in peace. I told Howard that the first meeting would be at the community center the following night.

"We'll be there," he said.

I knew I was in over my head, so I got a few older youth workers to run the group. Sure enough, Howard got his guys there, and before long something really good started to happen among those kids. Some of them dropped out right away, but some of them responded to the gospel. Howard, the leader of the gang, was the first to make a decision for Christ. By the time I went back to college, he and I had become close friends.

Howard was serious about following Jesus. Everybody in the neighborhood saw the changes in his life. He gave up drugs and alcohol. He went back to school. He did not break free of his gang altogether, but he began to influence his friends much more than they influenced him. Howard even volunteered as a Bible study leader with the same little kids he had been disrupting the summer before. When he graduated from high school the following spring, all of his youth workers were as proud as could be.

By that time, Howard had developed a serious relationship with a young woman in the neighborhood, and so he turned his attention to getting a job so that they could be married. That was when everything went bad. Try as he might, Howard simply could not get a decent job. Part of the problem was that, despite his diploma, he was barely literate. Part of the problem was that he was too proud to wash cars or flip burgers, knowing he could never support a family that way. In any case, the longer he looked for work, the more depressed he became.

Then one day Howard stopped coming to youth group and started showing up on the corner with his old friends, doing the one job he knew that paid more than the minimum wage. His youth-group leaders went up there to talk with him, but he just turned away from them, embarrassed and ashamed that he was selling drugs after all. And then one night a deal went wrong, and the men in the car came out shooting.

Howard ran through the projects, trying to get away, but they chased him into one of the buildings and caught him up on the roof. They beat him up there, and then they threw him off that roof and onto the playground, where he died in front of some of the same little kids who had been part of his Bible study group.

When I found out Howard was dead, something inside of me died as well. In that moment, all the joy of Howard's conversion and growth disappeared from my heart and was replaced by frustration. I had testified to everyone I knew about our inner-city miracle man, but I felt like a liar now. He had tried to make it as a Christian, but he had failed, or perhaps he had been failed. It did not matter then who was to blame. What mattered to me was that Howard's much-celebrated conversion came to nothing in the end.

I am not questioning Howard's eternal security, or anybody else's for that matter. All I am saying is that he did not get saved from the clutches of evil after all, as far as I can see.

We have lost more kids since then, of course. Joey, who as a high school sophomore led all his buddies to Christ, only to get snatched away two years later by some race-baiting cult leader. Kele, who got clean and sober at eighteen, just in time for some sexual predator to turn her into a prostitute. And Raymond, who assaulted a girl in his freshman dormitory six months after we had moved mountains to get him into college at all. But even as the older ones kept falling through the cracks, we kept leading younger ones to Christ.

Slowly it dawned on me that, especially in this inner-city culture, it was easy to make kids professing believers in God. What is hard is making them into lifetime disciples of Jesus. Counting conversions, I decided, is a cheap trick to cover up a hard truth. And the hard truth is this: The streets are full of danger for a fresh convert, and we Christians lose a whole lot more people than we win down here.

FOURTEEN

Patience Is a Virtue

Every August I travel around the country visiting as many Mission Year closing retreats as I possibly can. The official reason I show up is to encourage the young missionaries leaving our program to live out what they have learned in the city wherever they end up in the world. The personal reason I show up is to get stories. A guy like me is always on the lookout for stories.

Because our Mission Year people are so focused on building authentic relationships with their neighbors, most of their stories have to do with the people they love in their neighborhoods, especially the children. I do not want to offend any readers who are gloating parents or grandparents, but, let me tell you, our inner-city kids are just plain cuter than any other kids. Anybody who tells you otherwise obviously has not been here. Oscar's story, however, was not about a cute little kid. Oscar's story was about a mean old lady.

Oscar is a Hispanic young man from the barrios of Southern California who came to Mission Year straight out of college, because he wanted to give to other people the same gospel that had been given to him. He ended up being placed in a largely African-American neighborhood in West Philadelphia, which was hard for him at first. In many ways, Oscar did not fit in. He worked hard at becoming a good missionary, though, and in time that hard work was rewarded. Gradually he became part of this new community.

However, all was not well. There was still one part of Mission Year that Oscar absolutely hated: community service. This was no small deal, because community service is nearly half the program. The problem for Oscar was his particular community service job: He was working with a local agency ministering to the elderly poor, and the woman he had been assigned to visit absolutely could not stand the sight of him. Every time he went to her house to help, she would criticize and insult him from the moment he arrived until the moment he left. She told him she did not need his help. She told him to leave her alone. No matter how he tried, Oscar could not please this cantankerous old woman.

"Her name was Catherine, and she was mean," he told me as we talked together on the retreat. "The way she behaved really got to me. I began to hate her, which I knew was wrong, but I couldn't help it. Then I felt so guilty and bad about myself, because I came here to love people. I prayed about it a lot, but, to be honest, I still hated her."

Nevertheless, Oscar kept going back to see this hard-to-please woman. In her eyes, he could do nothing right. When he arrived, she berated him for invading her privacy. Then, on his first visit after Christmas, she practically screamed at him for going home for the holiday. Finally, she told the newly engaged young missionary that he was bound to be an awful husband. That was too much. Oscar lost his temper.

"You may be right about me, Catherine," he shouted at her. "I may be no good. But at least I won't be married to an old witch like you! You must have made your husband miserable! I bet he hated you!"

Strong words. Not what I would have coached him to say, but, he told me, she stopped cold and suddenly let out a choked little cry. With tears in her eyes, she shook her head. "Oh, no ... my husband ... he loved me so much. He was my boyfriend. He was my lover. Oh, how I miss my husband now." Then she was sobbing.

The anger drained out of Oscar. He walked over to Catherine and softly laid his hand on her shoulder as she cried. After a moment, he asked her if she would please tell him more about her husband. It was the right question. She looked up at him with bright eyes, and for the first time Oscar saw the old woman smile. She said she would love to tell him everything, if he really wanted to hear it. Of course he did.

"It was amazing!" he told me. "I sat down, and we talked together for a long time about her marriage, and about the rest of her life, too. Just that fast she changed from the meanest lady I ever knew into a beautiful person. From then on, everything was different between us. I visited her more often. We became friends. I can honestly say that I love Catherine now. And I know that she loves me, too."

It was a good story, but I still had one more question. Did Catherine ever explain or apologize to him for treating him so badly for so long? Oscar smiled.

"She said she didn't want to let someone get close to her, after being alone so long. She was afraid of having her feelings hurt. That's why she kept pushing me away, to see if I was for real. She said that it was hard for her to trust me, but that when I got mad and yelled at her instead of just giving up, she knew I really cared."

People do that sometimes, especially people who have been badly hurt. They push us away because they are afraid to embrace us. They make us keep coming; they make us keep proving our love, until they are sure of it. Until they are sure of us. Sometimes it takes a long time before we see any good come out of our giving to others. In this world full of brokenhearted people, patience truly is a virtue.

Of course, if Oscar and Catherine are any example, in some cases losing patience is a virtue as well. As long as you don't give up.

FIFTEEN

In the Air

Honestly, I did not mean to eavesdrop. I admit that I noticed the woman coming up the aisle of the airplane because she was pretty. And by the time the man got on the plane, I was concentrating on my writing, or so I thought. But halfway through that late-night flight from Chicago to Philadelphia, that young woman and the businessman beside her got loud.

At first I thought he was hitting on her, which bothered me; he was much older, and, besides, I could see his wedding ring between the seats. However, once I began listening in earnest (OK, so maybe I did mean to eavesdrop after all), I realized that nothing could have been further from the truth. In fact, she—Jennifer—was the one driving the conversation. Jennifer was a zealously evangelical Christian, and she was taking no prisoners.

There is something compelling about watching another believer share his or her faith with an intelligent nonbeliever. In a way it is like watching a chess match, where each player moves and countermoves to gain an advantage over the other. In this case, however, our young Jennifer was badly outmatched. The businessman seemed willing enough to talk with her, but I could tell that his mind was already made up. Moreover, it was obvious that he knew a great deal more about Christian theology than she did. Indeed, I could not tell whether he was indulging Jennifer because she was so attractive or whether he was trying to undermine her certainty for sport. Regardless, she plowed ahead.

The conversation started with creation versus evolution, but it soon turned to predestination and original sin. It was an awful thing to behold. He toyed with her, asking questions he knew she could not answer and turning her words around on her, all the while smiling with amusement as she struggled in vain to make a case for Christianity. Before long, I found that it was all I could do to keep myself from jumping in to try to rescue her.

As it went on, though, my feelings turned around. The businessman in front of me might be smug, I realized, but he was also lost. He had no faith in the grace of God. He was alone in this world, or so he thought, with no one to turn to for ultimate answers to the questions of life. Sitting there on that plane, I remembered thinking that way myself; I remembered it well enough to feel compassion for him. And as I did so, my compassion for my evangelical sister Jennifer turned to frustration, for she was offering this man nothing that he really needed.

I began shouting at her in my mind: *Stop sharing your half-baked theology, sister, and start sharing your faith! Tell him why you need a loving God, and what it feels like for you to pray. Tell him what Jesus means to you. Tell him how your life has changed since you started believing in eternity. Make your relationship with God sound valuable, like a pearl of great price!*

I went on and on, saying nothing out loud. *Jennifer, he isn't interested yet, but maybe you can make him interested. Stop answering his questions, and ask him a few of your own. Ask him what he does believe in. Ask him what he is afraid of. Ask him how he feels about his work, what it means to him. Listen to him describe his life without Jesus, so you know what's missing. Then you can tell him what you have experienced of God yourself, instead of reciting what somebody else said or wrote.*

She kept theologizing until the plane landed and we all went home. He heard nothing about her life, nor she about his. I never said a word to either one of them, which makes me either polite or a coward or maybe a bit of both. All I know for sure is that as I walked away from those people, it suddenly struck me how seldom Christians like me ever really share our faith, especially here in the inner city.

We share our theology and our morality and sometimes even our love and resources, but hardly ever do we drop the invisible curtain and share what it is really like for us to follow after someone we cannot even see. Why is that? Why do we hide from people precisely that part of our lives that matters most?

A friend of mine tells me he thinks that to share our true faith would require us to admit how little we really have. After all, he says, to honestly talk about the experience of trusting God, a person must also be willing to talk about doubting God. About not understanding all the pain and poverty in the world. About not understanding the Bible sometimes. About wondering if he or she might have it all wrong. Perhaps my friend is right.

But perhaps there's a deeper reason we do not share our faith: Maybe we are afraid that other people are not as interested in our lives as they are in our ideas, when in fact just the opposite is true. The more I talk with my friends and neighbors, with my family and the folks sitting around me on the subway, with church elders and drug dealers and everyone else I meet, the more aware I am that our lives—and their lives—are just about the only things other people are really interested in at all. It may not seem that way at first, but underneath their hard exteriors most people are desperately eager to connect, to know and be known, to find out whether what matters to you might be important to them as well.

The problem is that even though we want to connect, most of us do not know how to listen and talk with one another about things that matter, which I think is the deepest reason of all that we do not share our faith. We do not know how to ask or respond to questions about values and motives, feelings and relationships, the way we know how to discuss things that are outside of ourselves, such as sports or the weather or even theology.

All of those reasons only get bigger when people from somewhere else come to the inner city. Here they want to seem more certain, and here they are even more unsure as to whether anyone really wants to know them. And if listening and talking about things that matter is hard anyway, it feels nearly impossible to the outsider who can barely understand the language of the streets, let alone the culture. Perhaps that is why most of those outsiders seem to approach the men and women they meet in the inner city much the way our young Jennifer approached that businessman on the airplane.

So, then, our task is to learn how to share our faith, our real faith, with other people, some of whom seem completely different from us. First we must come to grips with that faith, separating our own personal experiences with God from our largely secondhand theological systems and accepting our doubts as part of the process. Then we must come to grips with our neighbors, recognizing that behind all those differences is in most cases a deep desire for genuine connection. Finally, we must learn to listen carefully and speak truthfully about our-selves and one another and about those spiritual things that matter most to us, instead of simply talking at each other about things that lie safely outside of us.

My prayer is just this: That the young missionaries we send out there onto city streets—and you and I as well—will better learn to share our real faith. So help us, God.

SIXTEEN

Bad News and
Good News

Every neighborhood gets visited by tragedies, both large and small. A house burns down. A son or a daughter gets arrested. A marriage falls apart. Too often, when such things happen, the people to whom they happen are left to suffer alone, which is one very good reason for a ministry like Mission Year. Above all, we send our young missionaries out there to love their neighbors, especially when and where there is trouble.

They feed hungry people. They listen to lonely people. They work hard to make things better in some of the world's most difficult places. But good and kind as they may be, they are certainly not the only ones in those places who know how to love their neighbors.

In the summer of 1999, the mother of one of our missionaries, Coury, died quite suddenly. She was a good mother who raised a good son. The news of her death crushed him, of course, and by extension every member of his team. Our city director, Dave Thompson, sat up with all of them that first night, and Dave told me later that he was struck by the true fellowship of their suffering, and the comfort it gave to their grieving friend. Dave was not surprised when the young team members pooled their meager resources the next day, so that one of them could fly home with Coury, to support him at the funeral. What happened next, however, surprised us all.

News travels fast in the inner city, especially when it concerns someone as well known as Coury. As a missionary he was way above average, which meant that he had made all kinds of friends in that neighborhood. The kids there especially loved this red-headed southerner who never seemed to run out of energy. They were the ones who found out first about Coury's mother, when they came by the house after dinner, looking for fun. By the next morning, however, everyone on the block knew what had happened.

They waited for a while, but before noon people began dropping by the house to express their sorrow. Most of them did not stay for long, but all of them said something kind. Outside, on the street, they did something more. Those young and old neighbors, whom Coury and his teammates had been giving themselves to all year long, simply and quietly took up a collection. The bills they gathered were small, of course, because nobody on a block like that one has very much money. Still, before dinnertime those neighbors had collected more than $100. Later, at the evening service, the team's very small church collected another $150-plus.

At first Coury and his teammates were uncomfortable, feeling that they should not accept such gifts from people they knew could ill afford to give them. Finally, somebody explained to them that such generosity is the way of poor people.

"In this neighborhood," they were told, "whenever a family loses somebody, the rest of us all pitch in, because we know there's always going to be some funeral bill to pay or extra food to buy for all the folks who show up or some such thing."

And so it was that the rest of Coury's team was able to rent a car and drive together from Philadelphia to Kentucky, to stand beside their friend at his mother's funeral. It was a sad day for all of them, of course, but they were glad to be there, and thankful for the neighbors who gave them that opportunity.

Yes, every neighborhood gets visited by tragedies, both large and small. I praise God that in at least some of those neighborhoods there are people who already know how to love their neighbors. I also praise God that there are others who are learning how, in the name of Jesus.

SEVENTEEN

Lost in Love Park

She was a thin black woman all alone. She was probably in her early thirties, a little bit younger than I was at the time, but it was hard to tell, because she was so disheveled and worn out. I know her name was Sheila, though, because I asked and she told me. And I know she was hungry at the time, because I met her while I was trying to keep her from eating at our after-chapel picnic in Love Park.

I should have known better than to set up our picnic there. It is different now, but back then Love Park was a well-known gathering place for Philadelphia's homeless community. Friends of mine used to sleep out there on a regular basis, to protest the city's new antivagrancy regulations and to make sure no homeless people were mistreated by frustrated police officers. I should have known better than to walk into Love Park with more than thirty fresh-faced young people, laughing and singing with our arms loaded with pizzas and soda pop that we had no intention of sharing.

Before I knew it, there was a crowd of older men and women pushing past our stunned missionaries, grabbing for food. When one of our volunteers tried to stop them, they became angry. They quickly surrounded him and complained. "You all say you are Christians, right? So how are you gonna come out here and eat in front of all us hungry people like that? That's all wrong!"

I ran over to intervene, moving the ragged group away from our clearly frightened and uncomfortable young people, explaining and apologizing all the way. Eventually, I promised those hungry men and women their own pizzas if they would just be patient and leave our group alone.

Much to my surprise, it worked. Slowly the homeless people walked back across the park to where they had been sitting before, to wait and see if I kept my word. They were still waiting half an hour later, when I finally brought over a pair of hastily purchased pizzas and began handing out slices. Their anger toward me was gone, but I still felt terribly awkward standing there among them, knowing that this pitiful act of charity was small and selfish. I think they must have sensed that I felt bad, because they began to speak kindly to me, offering words of thanks and encouragement. A few of them even asked me to sit down and talk.

I wish I could say that something wonderful happened, that underneath those grimy clothes and behind those broken teeth I found wise and thoughtful men and women who needed nothing more than a fresh start in life. I wish I could say it was different from all the other times I have sat down to talk with homeless people, but in truth it was not different at all. We had strange, sad, circular conversations. I listened most of the time, doing my best to understand what they told me. I asked questions and quoted Bible verses and pretended to believe things I knew could not be true. As usual, the only way I could end those conversations was to interrupt by praying out loud for my startled new friends. The picnic was nearly over before I worked my way free and walked back to join the missionaries.

That was when Sheila, who was the first person I had prayed with, caught up to me again. I was standing with one of our teams, laughing and saying good-bye, when she suddenly broke into the circle. She looked around first, and then she looked right at me. "Please," she said quietly, "I don't want to bother you anymore. I'm not asking for anything. I just want to sing you a song. Can I sing all of you a song before you go?"

We all hesitated for a moment. "Sure," I said finally, "of course you can." I introduced her to each member of the team, instructing them with my eyes to indulge her. Then she smiled at us, in that same shy way that the children often smile at our day-camp pageants just before they begin their solos. Suddenly her expression changed completely. Her face went blank, and then she slowly looked down. For a moment, it seemed that she was utterly lost. I almost thought she was going to disappear.

Instead, she sang Psalm 61. In that circle of strong, well-heeled Christian college kids, on a warm summer night, this dirty, hungry, exhausted little woman with stale liquor on her breath closed her eyes and sang in a soft, clear voice:

Hear my cry, O God;
    listen to my prayer.
From the ends of the earth I call to you,
    I call as my heart grows faint;
    lead me to the rock that is higher than I.
For you have been my refuge,
    a strong tower against the foe.
I long to dwell in your tent forever
    and take refuge in the shelter of your wings.

As she sang, she began to cry, but she managed to finish the song. When it was over, she stood still and said quietly, "I need y'all to pray for me." So we all held hands, and each of us prayed, thanking God for Sheila, reminding him of her life, and asking him to help her somehow, to give her shelter and peace.

With the last amen, she walked away—disappearing after all. We stood there in silence for a moment, and then those young missionaries left too, without a single word of explanation from me.

Since that picnic in Love Park, I have thought a great deal about our encounter with Sheila, and I am still not sure what it meant. I wish I knew where she learned that psalm, how those words were planted in her heart, and how they spoke to her in the darkness of her life. I wonder if she was in somebody's church day camp twenty years ago, and if that means some of the kids in our church day camps now will end up twenty years from now lost in Love Park, or some place just like it. I hope not, but I think so.

So what good does it do to teach them, if, after all, they end up drifting aimlessly through life? What good does knowing Psalm 61 do for Sheila? So what if she cries out to God for refuge, for a tent, for the shelter of his wings? He must not hear her. She sleeps hungry in Love Park.

And yet what if he does hear her? What if he is on his way? What if he is even now leading her to the rock that is higher than all of us? What if all she has to do to is hold on, though her heart grows faint, and trust in the love of God, though it still seems to be at the other end of the earth? What if all she has to do is live by faith?

Then, of course, it would do a lot of good for Sheila to know Psalm 61. And then our prayers for her that night may not have been in vain.

EIGHTEEN

Fight the Power

A few years ago I bought a subscription to a young people's magazine called *The Source,* which proclaims itself to be "the one and only independent voice of hip-hop music, culture, and politics." At first I merely skimmed over each issue, but then one day I sat down and took a long, hard look at *The Source,* and it nearly broke my heart.

Almost every page was filled with images of loveless sex, mindless violence, and endless materialism, which would have been bad enough except for the naive, pseudo-black nationalist rhetoric that held it together. Glowing articles about gangster rappers who denigrate women, letters extolling the virtues of being "all about da money," and editorials defending riot-driven looting, vandalism, and cop killing as legitimate political activities, all pretended to somehow promote the African-American community. The production values were incredible, and the writing was fresh and provocative, but in the end *The Source* seemed to me little more than a slick, angry, exploitative ode to sin.

Unfortunately, both *The Source* and the perspective it expresses are booming on the streets. Millions of inner-city kids are being sold a well-packaged, high-action, self-destructive lie, and it is costing a lot of lives. I see them on every street corner, dressed in expensive designer sportswear, drinking name-brand malt liquor, bobbing their heads to the latest beats, joking with one another and laughing as if they were on top of the world, when the fact is that the world is on top of them.

The problem is not that they cannot get what they want and enjoy. The problem is that what they want and enjoy are worthless material things and cheap temporary pleasures. Those kids on the corner are the ultimate expression of market-driven corporate values, the world's most perfect consumers. Bombarded daily by blatant images of wealth, sexual stimulation, violence, and personal pleasure, they have been seduced away from those nonmarket values—love, intimacy, service to others—that are the true stuff of life. Like so many Esaus, they have been systematically duped into trading their birthrights for hip-hop bowls of porridge.

What bothers many people I know about all this is the danger posed by a generation of soulless young people willing to do whatever it takes to get what they want and do what they enjoy. Certainly that danger bothers me as well, particularly because my family and I live in the city. The drug culture here especially frightens me, because I have seen firsthand the way crack cocaine robs men and women of their humanity, so that nothing else matters to them but getting another fix.

A few years ago I interrupted an addict in the process of stealing my car battery. I thought he would drop it and run, but he just looked at me like a wild animal ready to fight for his life, and I ran instead. His eyes told me he was a desperate junkie who would not think twice about killing me to get his high.

Of course, to teenagers and young adults growing up on the streets, money and the social acceptance it buys can be as powerful as any drug high. That is the true genius of advertising, I suppose: to make a pair of sneakers or a new cell phone seem more valuable than the life of another human being.

What bothers me even more than the danger they present, however, is what is happening to these young people themselves. All these things they have been taught to want and enjoy are destroying inner-city kids much more efficiently than these kids can destroy anything else. It is easy enough to stop the crimes of juvenile delinquents by locking them up, but how do you replace a young woman's lost soul? How do you restore a young man's lost humanity?

I know this much. The gospel is the beginning of the answer. Our message about a powerful, loving God who redeems the world through the sacrifice and resurrection of Jesus Christ is as ultimate and relevant today as it ever was and always will be.

Even so, the gospel doesn't feel all that ultimate and relevant when you are trying to screw up your courage to start talking to those hip-hop kids on the corner. Much as I hate to say it, it is awfully hard to know where to start with young people who increasingly do not care about the nonmarket values—love, intimacy, service to others—that our faith promises to deliver. They read magazines like *The Source* instead of the Bible for a reason.

The most obvious course of action is simply to repackage our message so that it appeals to young people on their own terms, which is one reason why hip-hop Christianity is exploding all over this country. Right now it seems as though somebody is producing a Christian version of just about every aspect of urban youth culture, from music to sportswear to television shows. Gospel rap, hip-hop, devotionals, and funky WWJD sportswear are big business these days. Indeed, just the other day a fellow called me to promote a magazine he says is intended to be the Christian version of *The Source*.

Unfortunately, such glitzy Christian consumer goods will never be able to compete with the no-holds-barred stuff produced by market-driven corporations for inner-city kids obsessed with wealth, sexual stimulation, violence, and personal pleasure. Our values may be the true stuff of life, but there is no way we are going to beat this world at its own consumer marketing game. We must take the competition to a higher level.

Repackaging the gospel is indeed the answer, but that repackaging has to be about the people who bring the message. The only way to defeat the loveless sex, mindless violence, and endless materialism that has so effectively captured the hearts and souls of so many inner-city kids is to show those kids the love of God as it manifests itself in real life. The only way to challenge them to reassess what they want and enjoy is to aggressively and consistently confront them with people who want and enjoy better things, and who are obviously and joyfully better off as a result. To make an impact, we need to love inner-city kids enough to be with them where they live, talking freely about what it means to us to live by faith, giving the gospel a chance to overpower all those other messages by the sheer force of its truth.

I do not mean that all of us are called to live in the inner city, but certainly all of us are called to care about those young people who are growing up there, surrounded by the hype and false advertising of a market-driven consumer culture. They are of infinite concern to God, after all, so we who love God must look after them as well. We must do our best to provide those precious children with what they need, which in this day and age means providing godly people who are ready, willing, and able to make the gospel look as good as it is and to show up this world as a liar. After all, the real Source is not a magazine.

NINETEEN

The Lady in White

People are often surprised that I do not own a car of my own. I like to act as though it has to do with my commitment to the simple lifestyle, or my concern for the environment, but the real reason isn't so noble. A few years ago my battered old Volvo finally died on me, and I simply never got around to replacing it. I meant to at first, but after a few weeks of borrowing my wife's van and getting around town on public transportation, I realized I need not bother. Besides saving the expenses of buying, maintaining, and insuring a car, I found I enjoyed riding subway trains and buses with the rest of the carless masses. Besides, because all of our young urban missionaries are required to use public transportation, I figured that this would be a great way for the boss to demonstrate some serious solidarity. And so it is.

But when I am wedged in the back of a crowded bus on a steamy summer day, forced to listen to the rap music pounding from the boom box of the same sullen teenager whose elbow is lodged in my ribcage, public transportation does not seem quite so ideal. Likewise, I have developed aversions to screaming children, highly odoriferous seatmates, aggressive panhandlers, and especially to seemingly knowledgeable direction-givers who in reality have no clue which route goes where. On the other hand, the worse it gets out there, the better the stories I come home with.

"This train is going straight to hell!"

I looked up from my newspaper, startled by the screaming voice as the subway pulled away from the Broad Street station. There, holding fast to the silver pole in the middle of the train, stood an older woman dressed in white from head to toe, with an expression of unbridled fury on her chiseled ebony face. She paused for a moment and then screamed again.

"This train is going straight to hell, and every one of you is going with it!"

I looked around me at the other passengers, every one of them staring at the woman dressed in white. They were the usual subway mix of laborers, students, mothers and children, and vagabonds. The whole scene seemed to me like something out of a movie.

"Repent, you sinners!"

The woman screamed again, her eyes darting wildly around the train. It seemed she was searching for someone upon whom to vent the fullness of her wrath. It must have seemed that way to the other passengers as well, because one after another averted their eyes to avoid meeting hers. Suddenly she pointed a long, white-gloved finger at me.

"You there, young man! Are you washed in the blood of Jesus Christ? Are you saved?"

I did not know whether it was safer to speak or keep silent. The other passengers were smiling now, nodding at each other as if to say, *Better him than us.* I tried to save myself.

"Yes, ma'am, I am," I said with as much confidence as I

could muster. "I am a born-again Christian." *That should do it,* I thought, silently congratulating myself for throwing in the key phrase *born-again.* Wrong.

"Then why are you just sitting there? Why aren't you warning these heathen about the coming judgment of God? Why aren't you telling them they're evil? Because you are evil too, that's why! You better repent yourself! All of you sinners on this train better repent!"

The train stopped again, the doors slid open, and, with one last look of scornful disgust, she was gone. Those of us left behind breathed a collective sigh of relief, and then we laughed out loud. "Dag, that lady was cra-zee!" "Where did she come from?" "Whooee, I'm glad she picked on you!" As the train rolled on, we swapped stories and made fun of the various religious fanatics we had all encountered in our travels. Part of me felt disloyal, because, of course, most of those religious fanatics we made fun of were Christians. And so am I.

Later, walking home from the station, I thought about that strange woman on the subway, and about the things she said. It occurred to me that I did not fundamentally disagree with her theology. I believe we are all sinners. I believe we are saved only by the blood of Jesus. I believe God judges evil. I believe people need to repent.

Perhaps, I thought, *that woman is on the right track after all.* She may not be effective, but at least she is standing up and proclaiming to the lost their need for salvation, while I am content to sit idly by and read my newspaper. At the same time, though, I knew there was something very wrong about what had happened on that train. I knew there was a reason why I was so embarrassed by my Christian sister, and why everybody else was so turned off. And I knew what it was.

She forgot the love. What she said and the way she said it made it perfectly clear to everyone on that train that it was no skin off her teeth if we all went straight to hell, so long as no one could say she didn't warn us. Worse than that, she acted as though God himself had no particular love for any of us, either. Her gospel was not good news at all. Like practically every street preacher and hit-and-run evangelist my subway friends and I had ended up ridiculing, that woman was more concerned with making people aware of their unworthiness than with convincing them of God's boundless grace and eagerness to forgive.

The more I thought about it, the happier I became with my own gospel, and the more grateful I became that I knew better than that crazy woman on the train. *Yes*, I told myself, *the problem is that there are too many people out there preaching hellfire and damnation, when what this sin-sick world really needs to hear about is the wonderfully tender love of God, expressed to us in the person of Jesus Christ.*

Only then did it hit me: People like me, who believe above all in God's grace, tend to leave the subway trains to the crazy ladies. We seldom climb up on milk crates in the middle of busy sidewalks and proclaim to those who pass by that Jesus will never stop loving them no matter what they do. We are not prone to scream at the top of our lungs, "The God of the universe wants nothing more than to embrace you forever!"

As surprised as they are that I do not own a car of my own, I think people would be even more surprised that over the past few years I have slowly begun to develop my chops as a street preacher. Even as I move away from speaking so often in churches and at Christian festivals, I find myself speaking more and more on subway trains and in bus stations. I have not yet dressed all in white, and I seldom raise my voice very loud, but there is no question that that crazy woman on the Broad Street line inspired me after all.

TWENTY

Between Happy Endings

My wife usually answers the telephone at our house, because she is better than I am at communicating irritation without being rude, and because she is faithful to protect me from all but the most persistent telemarketers. As she well knows, I hate talking on the telephone even when I really like the person at the other end of the line. So I was puzzled a few years ago when our phone rang late in the evening and all Marty said was, "Hello? Sure, Bart's right here."

"Hello. This is Bart," I said hesitantly, after she handed me the receiver. "Who's calling?"

"Uh, well ... this is Tyrone. It's been a long time, Bart. I hope you still remember me."

I remembered the voice right away, and would have even without the name, but it still took me a long moment to respond. You see, although I often tell his story, I had not heard from my old friend in more than ten years. "You know I remember you, Tyrone!" I finally said, with a smile in my voice. "I just can't believe you are calling me after so long. What's happening?"

He laughed. "A whole lot, man. Too much for the phone. I'd really like to see you, though. You got time to get together?"

I made time, the same way I would make time for my best

friend. Tyrone Murphy, after all, was the fourteen-year-old kid who kept me safe and showed me what ghetto life was about when I first came to the city as a naive college student. Tyrone was also the first inner-city kid I ever introduced to Jesus, and the one whose unbearable burdens first broke my heart.

Hanging up the phone that night, I realized that I had been in this ministry long enough to know that he was about to break it again.

We met for breakfast at a diner. He was a full-grown man, but still as playful and well-spoken as ever. Indeed, the way we fell to talking and joking around with each other, it was as though no time had passed between us. But time had passed, and we both knew it. Before long we were talking about what had gone on in our lives in the ten years since we had last been together. I went first and kept it brief and on the surface. I had a feeling that I would end up feeling awkward later if I described the many blessings of my life in too much detail. When it was Tyrone's turn, however, he let it all hang out. I was grateful that he felt he could still be so open with me after so long, but his story was hard to hear.

Tyrone had fathered a son out of wedlock. Later he had dropped out of school and sold drugs for a living, only to end up in jail. He had fathered two more children by another woman, with whom he was living now. He had also gone back to prison, this time for killing another man, but was eventually released, the court having ruled that he had fired his gun in self-defense. Now he was working a hotel job for minimum wage, trying to get himself and his life back together.

Listening to Tyrone describe all of these things was like having a nightmare. I had expected to be disappointed, but drugs and jail and killing were more than disappointing to me. But at least he did not insult my intelligence or my experience by trying to play the victim. On the contrary, Tyrone blamed no one but himself. He knew that he had had an opportunity to become something infinitely better than he was now, and he knew that he had thrown that opportunity away. He apologized for letting me down. He said that he had looked up my number and called me because now he wanted to change his life, because now he wanted to live like a Christian again.

We talked about all that for a long time, making plans for the future and promising to keep in touch with one another. We even prayed together in my car before I dropped him off at his house. But when he was gone, I did not feel hopeful. I felt empty. Looking back, I still feel empty.

Even as we were talking in the diner, I knew Tyrone's heart was not really into turning his life around. I think he meant what he was saying at first, but he seemed to get tired even thinking about all the sacrifice and self-discipline it was going to take to make it back to the high road.

Tyrone kept saying he had never lost his faith, that he knew all the missed bullets and mistrials were God's way of keeping him alive for some special purpose. But I wonder: Does God really work that way? I think about all the destruction and suffering Tyrone caused, about all the wasted time. I think about that other young man he killed, about his life and his faith. I think about Tyrone's children, growing up in the same kind of chaos their father knew as a child. It all seems out of control to me. I must confess that I do not see God's hand at work in quite as many places as some people.

The story I always tell about Tyrone happened when he was

a boy and ends with him as a committed Christian. His real story is still happening, though I hope and expect that it will end with him a Christian as well. It is what happens between those happy endings, however, that continues to trouble me.

I sometimes wonder why God doesn't just bring someone like Tyrone home the moment he surrenders his life to Jesus, instead of leaving him here to lose his will and get into trouble. Then I wonder why he doesn't just bring me home, too. God knows, when I think too much about what I do in this world, I am ready to go.

TWENTY-ONE

Making Hearts Sing

I do not fully understand the Book of Job, or much trust those who claim they do, but that does not keep me from reading it. On the contrary, I am strangely drawn to Job. Like a motorist passing a car wreck, I cannot help myself. Job's destruction is frightening, but I have to look.

One morning when I was looking, I was surprised to find something strangely inspirational in all that wreckage, something I had missed before, which was Job's wistful remembrance of the time before his trials.

> *How I long for the months gone by,*
> *   for the days when God watched over me,*
> *when his lamp shone upon my head*
> *   and by his light I walked through darkness!*
> *Oh, for the days when I was in my prime.*

JOB 29:1-4

Back then, of course, Job was the great and righteous man who most of all delighted God. Blessed in every conceivable way, Job led the good life, which I always took to mean that he simply sat back and enjoyed his wealth and comfort. But what I found that morning was that Job's own understanding of that good life had little to do with luxurious self-indulgence. Instead, as he described it, his prime was all about the glories of doing good for the helpless and unfortunate. All the respect he enjoyed from others, and even his own sense of personal well-being, was rooted in compassion.

When I went to the gate of the city
and took my seat in the public square,
the young men saw me and stepped aside
and the old men rose to their feet;
the chief men refrained from speaking
and covered their mouths with their hands;
the voices of the nobles were hushed,
and their tongues stuck to the roof of their mouths.
Whoever heard me spoke well of me,
and those who saw me commended me,
because I rescued the poor who cried for help,
and the fatherless who had none to assist him.
The man who was dying blessed me;
I made a widow's heart sing.
I put on righteousness as my clothing;
justice was my robe and my turban.
I was eyes to the blind
and feet to the lame.
I was a father to the needy;
I took up the case of the stranger.
I broke the fangs of the wicked
and snatched the victims from their teeth.

JOB 29:7-17

Magnificent images, are they not? Job does not long for wealth or power for their own sakes. Job does not lament even over his lost health or personal welfare. Instead, he fondly recalls the way it felt to walk into the center of town known primarily as a crusader for righteousness, as a rescuer of the weak and the oppressed. Is it any wonder that God delighted in such a man, for whom the good life was all about translating his own blessings into justice and kindness for people in need? How could anyone but Satan *not* love Job?

Every time I read those verses now, I practically jump out of my seat. I want to be that kind of person! I want everyone who calls himself or herself a follower of Jesus to be that kind of person!

The other day, a homeless old woman, who for years has fended for herself alone on the streets of Oakland, became angry and upset with our program director there, because the woman mistakenly believed one of our missionaries, who had become her special friend, was going to be sent home early.

"Don't make him go!" she cried, "I need him! He's good to me!" Her words were not exactly "he made my heart sing," but they were close enough to make *my* heart sing.

Over and over again I am reminded what a blessing our young missionaries are to poor friends and strangers alike in the inner city. And they are not the only ones. The world is filled with people who are learning to love their neighbors. We may not all be Jobs yet, but by the grace of God I believe we will get there.

TWENTY-TWO

The Purple Orchid

A few years ago I flew out west to preach in one of those new-fangled megachurches. You know the kind, five thousand members, with parking lot attendants, and stadium-sized video screens behind the pulpit, where all three morning services are choreographed down to the last minute. It was a lot of fun, actually, talking to so many people genuinely interested in matters of faith. I chose to talk about how one way to love God is by sacrificially loving his children. The great joy of Christian service, I told those megamembers, is that sometimes God is able to use us to change other people's lives in wonderful ways.

After the second service, a beautiful young woman, obviously pregnant, came up to the front of the auditorium and gave me a big hug. "Hey Bart," she proudly announced, "I'm from Philadelphia, too!"

"What part of town?" I asked. She looked wealthy to me. I expected her to mention a fancy neighborhood, such as Chestnut Hill or Mount Airy.

"I grew up in South Philly, down near the airport on Passyunk Avenue," she replied. "Do you know Jerry's Corner?"

"Sure I do," I said a bit too quickly, and then I smiled in embarrassment. Jerry's Corner is a notoriously seedy part of town, dominated by a cheap-looking strip bar. I drive that way often enough to know the name of it, though I did not tell her that.

"My name is Patty," she said, "and I used to dance there at the Purple Orchid."

I tried not to act surprised, but it was no use. In that sleek, suburban church on that bright Sunday morning, even the *idea* of a big-city stripper seemed so out of place. Still, there was no way she was kidding. Finally, I asked the obvious question. "How did you ever get from there to here?"

She smiled, looked me straight in the eye, and told her story.

It seems that Patty had been pregnant once before, back when she danced at the Purple Orchid. "I had a beautiful baby boy," she said with pride, "but his father was just what you'd expect in that situation. He wasn't as bad as some, but he was bad enough. One day he gave me a hundred dollars and told me to go buy some toys and diapers. I knew I had to get out of there, so I took the money, the baby, and ran."

She took a bus and ran all the way to Michigan, where her mother's sister took her in. Before long she started stripping again, just to pay the bills. Eventually she succumbed to drugs and alcohol. In her own words, Patty was a "hard partier," on the fast track to destruction. When I asked how it was that she managed to escape all that, she smiled again and pointed to the handsome man who had walked up to stand beside her.

"This guy here got me out," she said, taking his arm. "Bart, meet my husband, Phil. This is the person God used to save my life."

It turns out that Patty's husband had been a born-again police officer in Michigan who tended to talk about God a lot while on duty. He had met Patty on the job, but even so he did not treat her like the wild woman she was. Somehow, he looked past everything else about her to see the person Patty could become by faith and love. And then, slowly but surely, he helped her to become that person. And adopted her son in the process.

Unfortunately, I missed out on hearing the details about how Phil and Patty formed a family, left Michigan, and ended up as Bible study leaders in that particular church. The third service was just about to start, and in a megachurch time waits for no man, including the preacher. Still, I got to hear what Patty came up to tell me in the first place: "I just wanted to let you know that what you said up there is true. God really does use people to change other people's lives. I know it's true because it happened to me."

I have no idea whatsoever what I preached in that third service, but I know it must have been inspired, because *I* was inspired! I still am inspired!

What a great God we serve, who is able to do such wonderful things in and through his people! What a privilege it is to receive, to witness, and sometimes even to get to participate in his works of creation and redemption! But even as Patty's story fills me with joy, it also makes me think.

I am an urban missionary. Every day I work hard to make good things happen for inner-city people, trusting above all in the saving power of the gospel. Yet every time I drive by Jerry's Corner, I practically sneer at that dirty little bar, feeling nothing but contempt. I have no compassion for the people inside the Purple Orchid. The men there both frighten and disgust me, though surely they must be weak and unhappy. As for the women: Well, if I am honest, I must admit that I look at them more the way those other men do than the way Jesus does. In my lust, I ignore their confusion and degradation and forget to view them with the respect befitting sisters or daughters. It never occurs to me that they are waiting to be saved.

But now I need to know better, having met Patty and Phil. The next time I drive by the Purple Orchid, I need to give thanks for the true fact that sometimes God uses people like you and me to change other people's lives in wonderful ways. And I need to pray for the men and women inside who are lost, and to hope against hope that each one of them will be found, the same way Patty was found.

In this ministry there are always more defeats than victories. There are always more bills than dollars. The statistics are grim. And yet we do not despair, because the stories that defy those statistics are so wonderful. We do not give up hope, because each one of those stories is connected to that biggest and best story of all time. Life conquers death. Love conquers evil. God conquers Satan.

Oh, to think that in sacrificing our time, our work, our prayers, and our money for the sake of others, you and I get to be part of that story. What a spectacular gift is this earthly life of ours!

TWENTY-THREE

Finding Ray

Our missionaries go door to door in their neighborhoods at the beginning of their Mission Year. When I talk about this, my audiences immediately conjure up images of Bible-thumping, tract-waving young people stalking inner-city streets in search of unsaved people to evangelize on the spot.

After all, who has not been targeted for instantaneous conversion at some point, whether by a Jehovah's Witness, a Mormon duo, a band of Hare Krishnas in an airport, or even a born-again Christian stranger wanting to make sure we are bound for glory? Having established no relationship with us, these people nevertheless feel duty bound to question our lives and convictions and to foist upon us their version of ultimate truth. For most of us, these occasional encounters are somewhat uncomfortable, whether we agree or disagree with the folks who initiate them. Certainly most of the college-aged men and women we try to recruit for Mission Year feel like that and would be loathe to sign up for any program that required them to work that way.

In fact, that kind of hit-and-run evangelization is strictly forbidden in Mission Year. When we send our young people out to go door to door, our goal is not for them to proselytize their new neighbors, but rather to meet them, because that is the first step in becoming part of any community. Typically pairs of team members will walk the streets in broad daylight, simply introducing themselves to people as the new kids on the block. Of course, because those new kids on the block usually look so completely out of place, people often ask them why they are there.

When we first started the program, many team members would say they had come as Christian missionaries to the neighborhood, which basically offended everyone for one reason or another. After all, nobody likes to be defined as somebody else's "project." Nobody likes to have his or her home defined by some outsider as a ghetto in need of salvation. Our young people were inadvertently sending the paternalistic message that they were superiors who had come with all the answers, which especially angered those church and community leaders who knew better. Unfortunately, once they said those far-from-magic words, *Christian missionary,* their actions and motives were under suspicion by some folks for the rest of the year.

Over the years, both our attitudes and our language have changed. Now we instruct team members to say simply that they have come to be part of the local church and the neighborhood, and to learn to be good neighbors. Also, because the word *Christian* is as loaded as the word *missionary,* we have taken to calling ourselves followers of Jesus, rather than Christians. The response we get now is remarkably different. While a lot of people do not like or trust Christians or Christianity, it seems that almost everybody admires and respects the life and teachings of Jesus himself.

Our young people are still aggressive, I think, but not so

much about evangelism as about trying to connect with and love their neighbors. Sometimes when they are going door to door, they will say nothing more than this: "Hello, Mrs. Johnson. It's us again. We just stopped by because we are going to be praying tonight back at our house. We wondered, is there something special you wanted us to pray for, for you or your family?" That brief request often has a strange way of disarming people, so that they feel free to talk about themselves. When the same young people come back later to ask about whatever they were asked to pray for or maybe even to help out with some need they discovered, real relationships develop. After a while, there is no need for our team members to go door to door any longer. They spend their time visiting friends instead.

Of course, not everyone responds well to them, no matter how careful they may be. And even the name of Jesus sometimes makes people angry. There are slammed doors and crude jokes and even threats from time to time. Jared, a young man who came from Southern California to serve with Mission Year in Oakland, told me of one day early in the year when he and his partner Tom were going around their neighborhood looking for prayer requests.

"Nobody seemed to want to talk to us," Jared said, "and, to tell you the truth, I was beginning to wonder if going around that way really made sense at all. It just felt corny to me, you know, for these two white boys from the suburbs to keep walking up to all these black people in their own neighborhood as if we belonged there, offering to pray for them."

Finally, on their way home, Jared and Tom decided to knock on the door of one last house, which was so dilapidated they figured it was empty. A middle-aged man, looking nearly as run down, opened the door. Jared told him their business. Before he could finish, however, the man exploded, "Get out! Both of you, get out of my yard! I don't want your Jesus! You're all hypocrites anyway! I don't want Jesus!"

They left him and went home. But they passed him on the street once in a while and always went out of their way to greet him kindly. Eventually Jared even managed to engage him in a civil conversation. They learned that Ray, who lived alone, was a Vietnam veteran. A few months later, when they were better known in the neighborhood, the team threw an ice cream party for their friends. On a whim they invited Ray. He didn't stay long, but that he came at all felt like a victory to Jared.

Jared got to know Ray even better once he started volunteering at the local rescue mission, where Ray ate most of his meals. Eventually he and Tom formed a kind of friendship with this very lonely man. They heard lots of stories about the painful encounters he had had with Christians over the years. They came to understand the anger he had expressed that first day. They made no effort to talk him out of it, either. One night, coming home from a big church dinner, the team passed Ray's house, where he was sitting alone in the front yard, his head down.

"I knew Ray didn't have much to eat, and it bothered me that he was out there like that on a cold night, so I just went home and heated him up a plate from all the stuff we had brought back from church. When I walked up and gave it to him, he got all choked up, and he kept thanking me over and over like it was the biggest deal in the world. After we talked awhile, he said, 'I love you guys ... and I'm starting to believe in Jesus.'"

Unfortunately, his starting to believe in Jesus did not keep Ray's house from burning down a few weeks later. Suddenly this already poor man became homeless as well. I wish I could matter-of-factly state that our team or their church immediately stepped up to find Ray a new home, but as is so often the case in ministry among marginal people, it was not as simple as that. As we euphemistically say, Ray had "issues," and we had limitations. Jared and Tom still saw him occasionally, but he was harder for them to track down once he had no place to call his own.

Still, according to them, Ray's spirit was not broken by this latest setback. His new hope was not destroyed. He talked more and more often about spiritual matters and continued to enjoy his relationship with Jared and Tom. In fact, as the time drew near for his two young friends to leave Oakland, Ray kept telling them that he wanted to write to them, even though he could not give them an address to write him back.

As I said, our Mission Year people are generally not allowed to engage in hit-and-run evangelism. The one exception we make to that rule is when their churches decide to do that kind of outreach themselves and ask our team members to go along with them. The team members usually do not like it much, but they have learned to trust and obey their church friends, who have been ministering in their neighborhoods for many years. Sometimes what is completely inappropriate for cross-cultural outsiders works very differently for local folks.

A few weeks before the end of the year, Jared was pressed into service that way on a Sunday afternoon. Walking down the street with a handful of church members armed with Bibles and tracts, he was suddenly surprised to see the familiar figure of Ray coming around the corner.

"Hey Jared!" Ray yelled. "How you doing, buddy?" Appearing to ignore the well-dressed parishioners, this homeless black man ran up and hugged the one young white boy in their midst. He did not ignore them for long, however. Observing their Christian literature, and guessing their intentions, Ray cut them off before they could even begin. "You see this boy here?" he announced, pointing at Jared. "Well, this is the only person I want to hear speak about Jesus."

It happens like that sometimes. People say exactly what they mean.

"I hope he didn't hurt their feelings," Jared said later, recalling the incident. "But still, I understood where he was coming from. I know they have been in that neighborhood longer than I, but he doesn't trust church people, whereas I'm his friend."

As I travel all over this country, I meet lots of men and women who don't trust church people for one reason or another. Some have been let down, rejected or neglected, or otherwise abused. Some have believed what they read in the newspapers or see on TV. Some are afraid of any kind of mass movement, no matter what it claims to be about. Still, like Ray, most of those people are happy to have a good neighbor and happier still to have a good friend.

I don't know what will happen to Ray. Nobody knows, including Ray himself. I hope he has food to eat, and I hope he finds a home. I hope his faith deepens, so that he believes in Jesus more and more. Many would say that is what we should hope for most. But, if I am honest, the thing I hope for most is that Ray finds some new friends to love him. For one thing, friendship is what started him believing in Jesus in the first place. For another, even if his faith does deepen, God knows it is not good for Ray to be alone.

TWENTY-FOUR

My Secret

Now I am going to share with you my deepest and most carefully guarded ministry secret. Yes, the time has come for me to reveal that crucial piece of knowledge, which has enabled me to live and work among the urban poor for so long without being overwhelmed by the injustice of it all. And here it is: I am a natural-born winner.

Had I been growing up in the ghetto, I would have escaped. Count on it. No matter what, I would have found my way out, and once out, no one and nothing would have ever pulled me back.

If my mother had smoked crack and my father had gone off to prison, or just gone off altogether, I would have gotten over it. I would have found someone else to raise me, or else I would have had to raise myself. I would have done it right, too, teaching myself manners and self-respect and instilling in myself a work ethic out of thin air. So what if I lived in a dirty little house filled with too many other children and too little food, with only a television set left on all day to baby-sit? All the more reason for me to get a job. All the more reason for me to get down to the public library.

In that library I would have taught myself to read and write, of course, never minding if the school in my neighborhood did not have enough qualified teachers or books or even metal detectors to keep me safe from harm.

And that job? You can bet it would have been good and legal, even if that meant earning no more than the minimum wage. Drug dealing would never have been an option for me, regardless of how much easy money there was to be made. Sure, all my friends would have been out there every day, working the corners, talking on their cell phones, flashing their guns, and buying all the latest styles, but no amount of instant gratification would have tempted me. The good life can wait, I would have told myself over and over again, at least until I graduate from college.

And graduate I would, you see, because graduate I did. The proof is in the pudding. Obviously, I have what it takes to succeed. I know I did not have to contend with any of those obstacles along the way, but I most certainly believe I could have. As a matter of fact, believing that is the reason I feel so confident in my role as a missionary, showing those who have fallen by the wayside the path to righteousness.

Of course, I also believe that if it were me in the ghetto, that "ghetto me" would have grown up thinking and acting the same way that this "privileged me" thinks and acts right now. I picture myself overcoming those dire circumstances possessed with all the intellectual, emotional, and spiritual resources required to do so, conveniently forgetting where such resources actually came from in my real life. In imagining this great escape from poverty and despair, I take myself for granted, instead of facing up to the obvious truth of the matter: that if it had been me in the ghetto, I would not be who I am at all.

All this—my deepest, most carefully guarded secret—is a lie

or, perhaps more accurately, a myth that I use to justify myself for being who I am and having what I have in this world. There is no such thing as a natural-born winner. I have been lucky, or, if I want to spiritualize the same thought, I have been blessed by God. Either way, there was a lot of outside help involved. Where would I be without my wonderful Christian parents and all the advantages that their money bought for me? Without my highly competent and equally dedicated teachers and coaches and youth pastors? Without white privilege and American citizenship? I have no idea really, except that I am pretty sure it would be someplace very different from where I am right now.

A friend of mine tells me to shut my mouth whenever I begin a sentence "If I were you..." "If you were me," he always interrupts, "you would do exactly what I am doing, for exactly the same reasons, because you would see things the same way I do, because, after all, you would be me." That kind of logic always slows me down.

Perhaps a lot of us missionary types need to slow down. Perhaps before we can really love people who are living as prostitutes, junkies, child abusers, drug dealers, alcoholics, criminals, and welfare parents, we have to get honest about the ways we really see ourselves in relation to those people, and ask God to help us see the truth instead.

TWENTY-FIVE

This Ain't the Navy

How do you keep going? In the face of such overwhelming odds and sadness, what enables you to try and try again? How do you deal with the defeats? As an urban missionary, these are the questions I am asked most often. I always answer them the same way. I tell a story. The names and particulars may change, but I always have a story.

I spoke in San Diego once, to a group of college students at a church near the big state university. It was the end of a long trip, and I was tired in that way that is not cured by a good night's sleep. I was tired of my life. Yet I went ahead and spoke, the way I always do. Afterward, while I was shaking hands and answering questions, I felt a hand tap me on the shoulder from behind. I turned around to face a young, well-dressed black woman.

"Hey there, Bart!" she said, with a broad smile on her face, "do you remember me?"

I froze for a moment, the way I always do when somebody asks me to remember a name. I have always had an atrocious memory when it comes to names, even when I know exactly who a person is. When I ran a youth group in Minneapolis, I covered for myself by calling everybody "Buddy" or "Cousin" or some such general nickname. Later, as a speaker, I encouraged people to introduce themselves to each other in front of me; then I would chime in by saying, "Chuck here (or Janet...) is an old friend of mine," as though I had known the name all along. This time, however, I was really sunk, because I felt sure I had never seen this woman before in my life.

She waited for a moment, and then she laughed. "Fool," she chided, "it's me ... LaTonya! LaTonya Jackson! Now do you remember me?"

Yes, I did remember her then, and I also knew why I had not done so right away. LaTonya Jackson, you see, had been a member of that youth group I ran back in Minneapolis, more than five years before. I did not recognize her partly because she was showing up in the wrong place. Mainly, however, I did not recognize her because she looked like a completely different person.

Back in Minneapolis, when a girlfriend from school brought her to youth group for the first time, LaTonya was a disaster. She was a large, unkempt teenager who spoke with a slur and refused eye contact. She hung in the back that night, and I doubted we would see her again, but there she was next week, and the week after that, too. LaTonya was tough and distant, but she was also hungry for love.

Over time, she opened up and became a popular member of the group, but even as she did so, we leaders began to pick up the telltale signs of abuse and neglect. One night I drove her home after a meeting. Inside her front door was a dark room filled with men smoking crack cocaine. I found out later that LaTonya's uncle, who dealt drugs, had been getting her high and sexually abusing her on and off since she was ten years old. It was no wonder LaTonya was so messed up.

LaTonya was part of our youth group until she finished high school. The summer before she graduated, on a camping trip in the Rocky Mountains, she responded to one of my gospel talks by coming forward to become a Christian. I knew that I should be overjoyed, but instead I found myself calculating the chances for survival of a barely literate, ungainly inner-city girl, with a history of drug abuse and molestation. Somehow she managed to graduate, however, just before I moved from Minneapolis to Philadelphia. I remember how excited she was that day that her church family of youth group friends and leaders were all there, even though her real family was not. I also remember how worried I was when she told me that she had signed up to join the navy.

I was worried, because I knew how many inner-city kids join the armed forces to escape from the streets only to find themselves unable to cope with the structure and authority of military life. I also worried because I knew that LaTonya had made it this far in her Christian walk through the support of our church in general, and one of our female youth leaders in particular. But off she went. I had not seen her since. But now here she was, standing right in front of me, as shiny and bright as a new penny.

LaTonya threw open her arms, and I hugged her tight. "What in the world are you doing here in San Diego?" I asked.

"I'm stationed here with the navy," LaTonya answered.

I stepped back to admire her, big and strong and perfectly groomed. "The navy," I pronounced, "has been good to you."

Her smile turned to a frown. "This ain't the navy, Bart," she countered. "This is the work of God." Then she explained.

"The navy is just like you think it is, and as soon as I started,

I fell apart. Before long I was in with the wrong people, partying like crazy and getting into all kinds of trouble. I don't know what might have happened to me, but then one day this girl in my unit came up and asked me if I was a Christian. Well, I thought about our church and about that camping trip, and I told her yes, I was a Christian, but so what? Then she invited me to this Bible study with some other girls, and I went. With their help, little by little I came back to God. Since then, everywhere I have gone with the navy, God has provided me with fellowship, and I just keep growing."

I was blown away. This was too good to be true, but true it was. We walked out to the church parking lot together. As we talked I discovered that LaTonya was getting out of the navy later that year. When I asked about her future, she told me she was planning to go to a Christian college in the fall. Recalling her struggles in high school, I offered to help her out by pulling a few strings with some Christian college admissions folks I knew back home.

"Oh, Bart," she laughed again, "I don't need your help. I have already been accepted and given a scholarship to a great little college in Indiana." She paused. "Listen, I wish I could stay longer, but I need to go. On Sunday nights I run a Bible study myself, for a small group of inner-city girls. I just stopped by to give you a hug and tell you I love you." Then she climbed into a car—her very own car—and drove away.

I got into my rental car, but I did not even turn the key. Instead, I just sat there in the middle of that parking lot, pounding on the steering wheel and shouting at the top of my lungs, "Hooray for you, God! Way to go! Hallelujah! Praise your name!" And in that moment, I knew why Jesus says that the angels in heaven rejoice all over again every time just one person comes to God. In that moment, all the overwhelming odds and sadness were forgotten, swallowed up in a sea of happiness at a miracle too wonderful for words.

Suddenly I was not tired of my life anymore. Suddenly I felt as though I could keep going forever. Sure, we lose people, way too many people, but we win them, too, or, rather, God wins them through us, and we get to watch. And when God wins one, and I mean really wins one, it makes for a really good story. And a good story like that can keep me going for a long, long time.

Forget statistics. A raised hand or a walk down the aisle does not mean a thing unless somebody's life really gets saved, just as a white dress and a pair of gold rings does not mean a thing unless a couple really gets married. What you get out of this ministry business is a handful of great little stories, which, if you look at them long enough, appear to be part of a much bigger, much better story, which ends up with all of us sitting pretty at the feet of God.

TWENTY-SIX

My Wild Ride

A few years ago I got lost in Oakland. I had just dropped off our city director, Josh Horner, at his house after a full day of training with the Mission Year teams in that city. I was driving to the Motel 6 near the airport when it happened. I got on the 880 freeway all right, but I headed in the wrong direction. When I got off to turn around, there was no way to get back on. Before I knew it, I found myself wandering around dark factories and empty warehouses near the waterfront, looking for some way out.

I stopped my rental car at a red light behind a big old station wagon, which turned left when the light changed. As I crossed the intersection, though, the station wagon suddenly wheeled around and pulled in behind me. I figured the driver had just missed his turn, but before long I knew that I was being followed.

I was not scared right away, but after a few minutes I realized that I was in real trouble. I tried driving faster, but it did no good. On one long stretch of roadway, I pushed the gas pedal to the floor, but when I looked in my rearview mirror, the station wagon was still right there, going just as fast. I slowed down again, and then stopped at another red light. Behind me in the darkness, the driver lit a cigarette, casting an eerie orange glow on a man's face.

For a moment I actually considered getting out of my car right there, to walk back and confront this fellow, whoever he was. "What's your problem?" I wanted to ask in the toughest West Philadelphia accent I could muster, "Don't you have something better to do?" Instead, I stepped on the gas and ran the light, hoping he would let me go for fear of getting pulled over by the police. No such luck. I ran four red lights in a row. So did he.

Finally, after being chased for nearly half an hour, I saw a sign that led me back to the freeway. I figured that I was home free then, but as I drove up the on-ramp, the mysterious station wagon stayed right behind me at seventy-five miles per hour. By then I was shaking and soaked with sweat. "God," I said out loud, "I don't mind dying, but I surely don't want to go out this way. I could really use some help about now."

Once on the highway, I planned to drive to my motel, but suddenly that did not seem like a very good idea. Even if I made it inside, I did not want this fellow to have any idea where I was staying. Then I saw a sign for the airport, and decided to go there and hope for the best. I waited until the last second to swerve onto the exit ramp, but the big station wagon stayed right with me. Then just ahead of me on the access road, I saw a police cruiser pulling slowly across the parking lot of a brightly lit convenience store.

I whipped my car right into the lot, flashing the headlights and honking the horn until I pulled up beside the policeman's door. As the window came down, I yelled out, "There's a car following me! I've been driving all over, but I can't get away and I am really scared!"

Just then, before the cop could reply, *boom!* The station wagon smashed into the back of my car, right in front of him. "What the heck?" said the cop incredulously, climbing out of his cruiser to check the damage. Then he looked into the station wagon, and suddenly his expression changed. He whipped out his gun and crouched, pointing it at the guy in the driver's seat. I could tell he was ready to shoot.

"Put your hands on the wheel!" he barked, walking up to driver's side window. With his free hand, the cop opened the door. "Get out of the car! Lie down on your stomach. Do it now!" Before I knew it, police cars were pulling into the parking lot from every direction, and cops were jumping out to surround the man on the ground. As I watched in amazement from my own car, they handcuffed my pursuer and pulled him to his feet. He was a big, strange-looking man with a warrior's face and a ponytail, and as he stood he was glaring right at me.

"What's your problem!?" the first cop yelled at him.

"He knows!" screamed the man. "Ask him! He knows! He knows!" Another cop asked him his name. "One! Oooooone ..." he spat. They shoved him into the back of a police car and shut the door.

Finally, after carefully checking over the station wagon, two of the police officers walked over to my car, where I was quietly having a nervous breakdown. I opened the door and got out to talk with them. "Do you know this guy?" one of them asked. "Did you do something to him?"

After I told him the whole story, he just shook his head. "I won't lie to you," he said. "You are lucky to be alive. That man is totally crazy. He was out for blood tonight ... and all we found in his car was a pickax and a tarp." I was hardly reassured.

The other cop asked me what I was doing in Oakland in the first place. I told him that I was the leader of a Christian organization, in town to train a group of young missionaries. The first police officer nodded his head, as though what I had said made everything clear to him.

"That explains it," he said matter-of-factly. "This guy must be demon-possessed, and he picked you out because he sensed you were a man of God."

Now I must admit that that was about the last thing I expected to hear from a big-city cop. As it turns out, that cop was a Christian, as were most of the cops who helped me that night. Once I got over the shock of it all, we had an amazing conversation right there in that parking lot.

They wanted to hear all about Mission Year, and when I explained it they were genuinely enthusiastic about our ministry. Between them they knew all the churches we work with in Oakland, as well as a few we probably ought to start working with. They thought it was great that we were bringing good young people into the city. One of them even invited me to speak at his church's youth group the next time I was out there. They also were excited to tell me how their faith worked itself out in their police work and how they thought more Christians ought to join the force.

We talked together like that until an ambulance arrived on the scene, and then it took four of those cops to strap that big, scary man onto a gurney for his trip to a jail-house mental ward. Watching him struggle, I was mighty glad I had not gone ahead and confronted him myself.

Everything seemed surreal to me until my new friends finally packed up and left me there in that convenience store parking lot. Then I fell apart all over again. I was still scared when I finally got to my motel that night. Then it hit me that it was no accident that those police officers were Christians.

I often struggle to believe in miracles, but on that night I have no doubt that the Holy Spirit led me to the same place he led those men, so they could save my life. God answered my terrified prayer that night, and the prayers of all those who have interceded for my safety. The Holy Spirit guided me to those policemen, and the Holy Spirit guided them to me, maybe because we were seeking that guidance and maybe in spite of the fact that we weren't. Either way, I am alive and grateful.

I tell people that they should pray for those of us who live and work here in the city as though our lives depended on it. Because sometimes they really do.

TWENTY-SEVEN

Inasmuch

Feeling safe and secure in my own bed, I woke up early that Sunday, knowing I had a long drive ahead of me. The church at which I was supposed to preach was far outside the city. I felt good as I showered and dressed in the warm air of that summer morning, thinking over the things I planned to say from the pulpit later on. As usual, I would talk about the love of Jesus and the needs of the poor; as usual, the people in the congregation would listen to me respectfully because I am an urban missionary, and later give me money to support my ministry. The people in the congregation would also feed my ego, by telling me how impressed they were by my willingness to live and work for God in the inner city.

I will not pretend that I do not like the way suburban Christians tend to react to me. I enjoy the status I derive from my image as a front-line soldier in the battle to save the city. Indeed, like most urban missionaries, I have a mendacious tendency to play up the negative aspects of my own neighborhood to impress other people with my own bravery and sacrifice. In the heat of the moment, especially when there is a large contribution at stake—or a stroke of admiration—I can forget that this only reinforces the very stereotypes many of my neighbors are struggling to overcome.

On this particular morning, I felt as though I deserved whatever

I could get from that faraway church. Just the day before we had wrapped up an especially great week of day camp, with hundreds of city kids having the time of their lives at a picnic in the park. Everybody had worked hard. It had been a long day for me. I had driven the kids home, returned the bus we had borrowed from the suburbs, and taken the train back into the city at midnight. Tired as I was, though, it felt good to remember all those kids having so much fun together, and to know that I had helped make it happen. Adjusting my tie in the mirror, I was pretty satisfied with what I saw there.

It was still and quiet as I walked across the street to where my car was parked. The driver's side door was unlocked, but I paid no attention. I often do not lock my car, so if someone tries to steal my radio he or she does not have to break my window to find out that it is already gone. When I opened the door, however, my heart jumped into my mouth. Somebody was lying there in the back seat.

I jumped back instinctively, startled and scared, but when I looked again I saw that it was just a drowsy-faced little boy, who had obviously been sleeping in my car. The implications of the situation, however, did not occur to me right away. For some reason, I was still frightened, the same way I am frightened when I try to catch an unpredictable mouse in my bedroom.

"You get out of my car!" I barked at the little boy. "Go on, you get out of there right now!"

He did not say anything. He did not even look at me. He just climbed up between the front seats and out of the open door and walked slowly away from me, down the street, a skinny boy, eight or nine years old, wearing torn sneakers, jeans, and a dirty T-shirt.

I wish I could say that I ran after that little boy, but I just stood there and watched him go. Eventually my heart slowed down, and I got in my car and drove away. It took me a few blocks before I realized what had just happened, and what I had done. Even then, I kept on driving.

As I drove, however, I began to wonder what was the matter with me. Why had I reacted so badly? How could someone like me, on his way to preach about love and compassion, have had so little of either?

I had been startled, of course, because the little boy had shown up where I did not expect him. If he had been at the picnic the day before, I reasoned, things would have been different. There, on my terms, I would have learned his name. There I would have cared for his needs. But when he invaded my space, I became angry and scared. Stripped of the predictable patterns of my ministry, I shut down.

I began to think about that boy, imagining the kinds of circumstances that would have caused him to be sleeping in a stranger's car in the first place. I wanted to believe that he was a normal kid, who had run away from his good home for the night just to scare his parents, but then I remembered the way he was dressed. I knew there was no happy story.

I also knew that I was no man of God. I may run a nice day camp or preach a good sermon or even give sacrificially of myself, if given enough time to consider it (and congratulate myself for it, as well). But in the heat of the moment, when my true self was tested, I ordered a homeless little boy out of my car and out of my life, to fend for himself on the mean streets of Philadelphia. And then I went to church.

I do not remember much about the rest of that Sunday morning. I expect that I probably preached just as I usually do, despite the fact that I felt like a complete and utter hypocrite. Frankly, if preachers begged off preaching every time they felt like hypocrites, there would be precious few sermons to speak of in this world. I know I did not turn down any contributions, either. What I do remember is that Sunday afternoon, driving around my neighborhood looking for that little boy, and never finding him.

Something spoke to me that day, and what it told me was that there is something very wrong with me, that I am lacking spontaneous love and compassion, that there is still within me a fear of need and a need for control that prevents me from being the person God wants me to be. If I did not know better, I would say that Jesus spoke to me. But I know all too well that it was not Jesus, because when I shouted at Jesus, he climbed out of my car and walked away without a word.

TWENTY-EIGHT

A Pair of Hearts

For our young missionaries, the hardest part of Mission Year is not the pervasive poverty. The hardest part is not all the theological questions that poverty invariably raises in the mind of anyone who really thinks. The hardest part is not the sacrifice or the danger or even the incredible hours of hard work the program requires. No, the hardest part for virtually everybody who sticks it out is living together with five or six other Christians in a small space for twelve months.

All year long we call it community living, but the fact of the matter is that genuine Christian community does not develop right off the bat. First there is the honeymoon period, just after people arrive in September, when everybody is enthusiastic and eager to please. For a few weeks, or even a few months in some cases, a seemingly random collection of virtual strangers, who have been thrown together under intensely difficult and alien circumstances, will bend over backwards to act like old friends and to avoid conflict at all costs.

"It's amazing!" they breathlessly tell their city directors. "We can't believe the way we have become so close so quickly. God has given us such love for one another. Already we feel like a family."

Then, as surely as death or taxes, the wheels come off.

Cramped together in close, far-from-luxurious quarters, people get tired of being cheerful and polite. People get tired of other people and especially of certain other people. People just get tired. All those other pressures—the poverty, the theological questions, and the hard work—gradually take their toll.

Generally speaking, nothing dramatic happens right away. Instead, a quiet cloud of tension settles over the house, slowly building until you can practically feel it the moment you walk in the front door. Still, in most cases, the tension remains nonverbal for quite some time. These young people define themselves as Christian missionaries, after all. They are here to solve problems, not to *have* them. And certainly not to *be* them.

Eventually, however, something or somebody explodes, and suddenly all kinds of anger, resentment, frustration, misunderstanding, confusion, suspicion, and baggage from home come out on the table and into play. The honeymoon is officially over.

"John keeps hurting my feelings." "Mary is always late." "Bill doesn't respect me." "Janet refuses to open up." "Jamaal and Ken are teaming up on me." "Nobody listens to me." "I can't handle all this arguing." "Bobby spiritualizes everything to get his way." "I doubt Jennifer is really saved." "I wish I could just go home." The list goes on and on. Then they really are a family. A dysfunctional family, of course, but a family nonetheless.

Then, and only then, is there any chance for these five or six individuals living together in the name of Jesus truly to become the body of Christ, and to show their neighbors how their faith relationships with God really work. As long as they are playacting at being perfect Christians with no relational problems, they are irrelevant. Once the gloves come off, however, they become living examples, one way or another.

Over and over again, we tell our missionaries that what happens in their household largely determines what happens in their ministry outside it. It is not simply a matter of being encouraged or discouraged by their teammates, we say. It is a matter of people knowing whether or not they are disciples of Jesus by the way they love one another.

Kris came to me first, back when I was a city director myself, in charge of all our teams. She was more experienced than most of our volunteers and especially good with younger children, because she brooked no disrespect. Like so many of the best teachers and parents in inner-city communities, Kris was tough and determined, and the kids loved her for it. Unfortunately, her teammates did not similarly appreciate her blunt manner, and on this hot summer afternoon I could see why.

"Listen, Bart, I do not want to cause trouble for you or anyone else, but I am afraid I just cannot work with Tamara. She has been difficult for me right from the start, but lately we cannot seem to agree on anything. I throw a misbehaved kid out of day camp for a week to teach him respect, and she lets him in the next day because 'we need to forgive.' I try to establish a chore schedule for our team, but she convinces everybody that we need to be flexible and trust each other to get things done. And the worst thing of all is that she walks away from me whenever I try to talk to her about anything." Kris paused for a moment. "I have prayed for patience, but it isn't working," she said. "I basically hate her now."

Later that afternoon, Tamara told me the same story from the other end. "Kris is a tyrant, and she has it in for me, because I don't automatically obey her every command. Nothing I do is right. I could handle her bossiness, but she keeps yelling at me in front of everybody, including the kids in the neighborhood. In my family, people don't yell. She's a total witch, and I'm sick of her!"

Tamara was just about ready to leave the program, which would have suited Kris just fine. Already the two were not on speaking terms, according to their poor teammates, who were caught in the middle and supremely unhappy about the situation. By the time we all sat down to dinner together, I realized that both the team and its ministry in that neighborhood were in danger of total collapse. I had no idea what to do about it, so I stalled for time.

"Please," I asked Tamara and Kris after a very awkward meal, "take a week and pray some more, both of you. You don't have to become best friends, but you absolutely must not give up on loving one another. This is a matter of biblical obedience. I hate to say it, but if you are not willing to keep trying with each other, I am going to have to send you both home."

I left that night fully expecting to have to carry out my threat. As devastating as it would be to everyone involved, to me there seemed to be no other choice. If we sent missionaries home for breaking our rules against dating and using drugs, how could we allow them to willfully disobey Jesus' commands to love one another?

I wonder what you call a miracle? Does a mountain need to move or a river stop moving? Does somebody need to be healed of a terminal illness? Here is what I call a miracle: Those two young women prayed, each for herself and the other. And when they were done praying, both of them were truly and painfully broken. Before they ever spoke a word to each other, God spoke a word of his own to each one.

For the first time in her life, Kris was confronted with the truth about herself in a way that she could not escape, and what she saw in that truth terrified her. Behind her bossiness and air of certainty, there were insecurities and family patterns that she realized were spoiling her life. Suddenly she knew that unless she could change, she was bound to be alone in life.

Tamara's issues were more complicated and still are less easy to describe. Suffice to say that her Mission Year team was effectively her first family of any kind, and that she bore the scars of having been emotionally left alone far too long.

I know these things only because Kris and Tamara told them to me, after they told them to each other. In his most gracious way, God not only showed them some very important truths about themselves, but also showed them enough of his love that they became able to love one another as well. Do not get me wrong. They remained two very different women with very little in common. But somehow in that miraculous week, they found a way to connect. By the time I came back over to resolve the situation, Kris and Tamara were a pair of broken-hearted but healing sisters in Christ.

Before long, of course, Kris and Tamara argued again. Too many things are happening all the time for people not to disagree about some of them. But this time, and all the times from then on, they argued the way people do when they love each other. Tamara stayed in the room. Kris learned to keep from raising her voice. Better still, along with the two of them, their entire team discovered that the sky did not fall in on them when they expressed their true feelings about things, so long as they were careful of one another's feelings as well. The dreadful cloud of tension disappeared, replaced by understanding and not a little bit of healthy conflict resolution.

That group turned out to be a very good ministry team, despite the fact that they had no genuine "stars." Frankly, in this kind of street-level work, genuine "stars" sometimes get in the way of the Holy Spirit. People love to be around such confident, talented, and attractive young men and women, but they do not identify with them the way they do with people like Kris and Tamara, who struggle in spite of their faith in God. As they and their teammates openly worked to love one another, their neighbors had the chance to see and talk with them about the great difference Jesus and his teachings are able to make in the lives of weak and fallible human beings. The distinction between missionary outsiders and needy insiders crumbled away, once that team finally began to form the real friendships this ministry is all about.

I think that same kind of breakthrough needs to happen in every Christian church and family and friendship, if we who believe in Jesus ever hope to make our faith attractive to those who don't yet share it. The people I talk to are not particularly interested in our theology and are not particularly worried about heaven and hell. What concerns them is whether something or someone out there can help them overcome their "issues" and teach them how to love and be loved in spite of the fact that they are woefully less than perfect. And what keeps them from thinking that we can help is that all too often we refuse to let them see us working hard at loving one another, or, worse still, we refuse to work hard at loving one another in the first place.

Christian community living is not just the hardest part of Mission Year; it is the hardest part of life, as well. When I think about it that way, I am more than glad we serve a God who specializes in miracles like the one he wrought between Kris and Tamara.

TWENTY-NINE

Against the Odds

I wrote another letter of recommendation the other day. I do that pretty often, actually, due to the large number of young people who pass through Mission Year each year, but this one was quite unusual. This one was a letter of recommendation for college admission for an inner-city kid I know in North Philadelphia who by all accounts had practically no chance of even graduating from high school. His name is Daniel Gonzales, but everybody calls him Pancho, and though his story is far from over, it is a good one nonetheless.

Like a lot of kids in North Philly, Pancho grew up surrounded by chaos. Both his folks are serious drug users. His father is a drug dealer as well, who has been in and out of jail. The details of his own descent are just that: details. Everybody in Pancho's neighborhood knows the basic plot, having already watched a hundred other Panchos live it out. Poverty. Neglect. Insecurity. Academic failure. Crime. Punishment. Reload. Repeat. Frankly, I get tired of hearing such tragedies. Besides, the important part of this story is not how Pancho got into trouble, but how he got out.

You see, there was this church near his house that opened a summer day camp when Pancho was thirteen. Why he checked it out, I do not know. Probably he came out of idle curiosity or sheer boredom. After all, there are not too many recreational options available to kids in that particular neighborhood during the summertime. The city pool there contains a bizarrely abandoned car, not water. Not many families can afford a vacation away. Regardless of why he came, I know Pancho stayed for that day camp because he really hit it off with one of the counselors.

Troubled though he was, Pancho was still an easy kid to like, blessed with a winning smile and a sly sense of humor. Before long, he and his counselor were hanging around together outside of camp as well, playing basketball and talking about God. By summer's end, Pancho had a completely different set of friends and a whole new identity. He was a Christian kid now.

Fortunately, a handful of laypeople from church started a weekly youth group that fall, so Pancho had a good place to develop. His new faith did not solve all his problems, of course, but it definitely made a difference in the way he approached them. Given discipline and attention for the first time in his life, this child of the streets began to blossom into a fine young man of God. He was not just a taker, either. Pancho had always been musical, but now he started writing songs about Jesus and singing in public for the Lord. His church's youth group grew, as well, in large part because of all the new kids Pancho brought along with him. I got to know him a little bit during this time, and there was no mistaking it: This guy had a great heart and a truckload of charisma, to boot. He was bound to succeed.

A few years later, I received an unexpected telephone call from Pancho's church. It was the young man who headed up the youth group, asking for help. It seemed that Pancho had dropped out of high school with failing grades and run away from home with no place to go. The pressures of his family situation had finally gotten to him, this primary youth worker told me, and now he and Pancho were sitting there at the church, desperately trying to figure out what to do next. Before I knew it, my youth worker friend put Pancho on the line.

"Bart, man," he said in a low voice, "I really want to make it. I don't want to mess up. I want to go to a Christian college and be a Christian singer or a youth pastor. I'm serious, man. I promise, I'll do anything to make it! A long time ago you said to let you know when I needed your help. Well ... can you help me now?"

I knew what Pancho was talking about. When I first met him, he had told me of his plans, and I had told him that when the time came, I would be happy to pull a few strings on his behalf. Honestly, given what I knew about his background, I never expected to have to deliver on that promise. Now Pancho and his youth worker had put me on the spot.

After practically an entire day on the telephone, it turned out that I could indeed help Pancho, but my help would certainly put his determination to the test. The only high-school-dropout string I could pull was at a strict, Seventh-Day Adventist boarding school, where I had spoken once, way out on the plains of Idaho. With his poor academic skills, his Bible-church theology, and his pure inner-city background, I figured Pancho was a long shot out there at best.

Somehow, he made it. Somehow the poor people in his church scraped together enough money to buy him a one-way plane ticket and even sent him off with a little bit of spending money. Somehow, the good people at that school managed to teach him how to be a student after all. Most amazing to me, that fun-loving kid somehow disciplined himself to do both his schoolwork and the campus landscaping work he took on to help pay his way. Semester after semester, Pancho passed. Moreover, surrounded by tall, blond-haired, blue-eyed country folks, this pudgy Hispanic street kid ended up becoming the most popular student in the school. He did more than graduate. He was homecoming king.

I did not hear from Pancho very often after he left for Idaho, but his youth worker at church kept me posted all along. Not surprisingly, Pancho's success out there was a major source of joy for the church family in North Philadelphia that had made it possible, and especially for those friends who are now thriving in the youth group because Pancho brought them there in the first place. Of course, Pancho's story gives me great joy, as well.

One reason I like his story so much is because Pancho is a great kid who was redeemed by God through an inner-city church that did its job. On some level, everything I have worked for over the past fifteen years, and everything I am still working for today, all shows up right there. Please, do not get me wrong. Our ministry did not save that kid. God did. It was God's will. And to do his will, God used Christian people from Pancho's own inner-city neighborhood, along with me and some Christian people from Idaho, because we were handy, I suppose, and willing to be used.

But it was a team from our ministry that got that first summer camp started, and it was our ministry that trained the church laypeople who started Pancho's youth group. Pancho's primary youth worker came through our ministry, too, which is how he joined the staff of that church in the first place. The bottom line is this: Our ministry worked! A genuine miracle happened up there in Philadelphia, one small step at a time, and

Mission Year had a little part in it. Against all odds, Pancho is going to college in the fall.

Which reminds me: I have a letter of recommendation I need to put into the mailbox. Hallelujah!

THIRTY

A Lesson from
Saint James

Jennifer left her neighborhood early that morning and took
the train downtown to hear a famous preacher scheduled to
speak that day, hoping for some kind of inspiration. It was late
March and her Mission Year was far from over, but she was practically worn out just the same. It is not easy living and working
with five other adults in a cramped house in the inner city even
when everything goes right, and for Jennifer and her teammates
that year in Chicago, everything had definitely not gone right.
They were not giving up, though, which was one reason
Jennifer was taking this day away. She intended to refocus herself on what she had come here for in the first place.

Happily, the famous preacher was as good as advertised and
well worth the trip. As a special bonus, the choir and the congregation were both positively inspired as well. By the time that
Sunday morning service was over, our Jennifer was flying high
beneath the wings of God's great and glorious love for his children. Her sense of purpose and hope was suddenly restored, her
commitment to Jesus clear and present in her mind. She walked
out of that church positively determined to share God's love
with any and all lost and needy people who happened across her
path from that moment forward. On a less spiritual note, she

walked out of that church hungry, so she headed straight for the nearest McDonald's, singing to herself all the way.

As Jennifer bought and ate her meal, flushed with the joy of the Lord, it occurred to her that surely there must be people close by who needed to experience God's love. Here and now was her first chance to put her resolve into action. It was a bitterly cold day in Chicago. As she prepared to leave the restaurant, Jennifer decided to purchase a large cup of coffee. Her simple plan was to give that cup of coffee, along with some kind words of encouragement, to the first cold-looking person she saw. She prayed that God would make her the best kind of blessing.

Outside again, Jennifer walked only a few steps before she saw a wild-looking man in a battered wheelchair, rolling straight toward the entrance. He was a black man, forty or fifty years old, wrapped in a worn and dirty army coat. His beard was long and bushy, his gray hair was everywhere at once, but his eyes were looking directly at Jennifer, a young white woman. She was a little bit scared, but she was excited as well. Smiling warmly, she moved toward him. Before she could say a word, however, the man in the wheelchair angrily addressed her.

"I know what you're gonna do!" he snarled. "You're gonna offer me that cup of coffee, aren't you?"

Jennifer smiled again, nodded her head, and held out her gift.

"Well, you can keep your —- coffee!" he barked. "I don't need any —- coffee! What I *need* is a dollar!"

She was stunned at first, and then she was angry. *Here I am trying to reach out,* she thought, *and instead of thanks, I get yelled at.* She withdrew the coffee and walked around the man in the wheelchair. Under her breath she muttered, "What you *need* is Jesus!"

The man wheeled himself around and shouted after her. "What's that you said to me?" he demanded.

She turned back to face him.

"You think I don't know Jesus?" he shouted. "Who do you think helps me push this wheelchair every day? Who do you think takes care of me out here? Jesus does, that's who! Just because I'm poor, you think that I don't know Jesus?" He reached out and pushed her away with both hands. "Go on, you; get out of here!"

Jennifer turned away sobbing, embarrassed and ashamed of herself for being so insensitive. She rushed along the sidewalk. The man in the wheelchair was absolutely right about her and she knew it. She had thought herself better than him just because she was better off. Now she was a mess.

Halfway down the block, the man in the wheelchair caught up with her. She walked faster, wishing she could disappear, but he stayed with her. Looking up at her, he spoke again, but this time his voice was soft.

"Why did you do that?" he asked quietly. Jennifer stopped and looked back at him.

"Because I wanted to show you that God loves you, and that was the best way that I could think of."

"Oh," he said. "That was your mistake right there. You think that the only way to show people love is by giving them stuff." He smiled and pointed at himself. "You need to take a lesson from old Saint James here. You want to know what I do? When I want to love people, I look 'em right in the eye and give 'em the biggest smile I can and say, 'Hello there!'"

Obviously, old Saint James was no longer angry with young Jennifer. Instead, it seemed he wanted to ease her pain somehow, to let her off the hook. He asked her name, and they talked awhile, mostly about their mutual faith in Jesus and about how Jennifer desired to love people mainly because of the way Jesus loved people first. It was a real and respectful conversation this time, between fellow human beings. Then Saint James said to Jennifer, "I know what will help you." He took her hands and bowed his head, as if to pray.

Jennifer smiled and bowed her head as well, expecting the usual Christian phraseology and biblical language, but at first there was nothing but silence. Then the older man began grunting acknowledgments, as if there were someone else on the other end of a telephone line.

"Un-huh ... yes ... OK ... I got it." After a few moments, he stopped and smiled up at her again.

"Jennifer," he said, "God told me to tell you something." He tapped on his chest. "You see, Jennifer, love comes from in here. It isn't things you give. It comes from your heart." He paused. "Listen. It's easy to love people ... but it's easy to hurt people, too."

Jennifer nodded.

"I love you, Jennifer," said Saint James.

"I love you, too, James," said Jennifer.

"Then how about you give me a hug before you go?" he said, and now there were tears coming down his face.

She leaned over and hugged him, and he hugged her back. Then they went their separate ways.

Jennifer told me about this particular singular experience in the living room of her team's apartment, months after it happened, one morning when I stopped in for a visit. She said that it defined her year and that the things she had learned from Saint James had utterly changed her life. I do not doubt her. After all, sometimes that is how the kingdom works.

AFTERWORD

What am I supposed to do with a book like this one?"

That is the question Owen Brock asked me, when he and Michael Wilson came out to take my photograph for the cover. Because he has been my friend for many years, Owen has often read and heard me tell these stories about the people and the ideas that inhabit my ministry. But now, having seen my stories laid end to end for the first time, he wondered what purpose I hoped they would serve for those who happened to read them. You may wonder the same thing. It is a fair question.

First and foremost, I hope these stories make you feel something, or, rather, I hope they make you feel many different things.

Some feelings are fairly predictable for those good people who stop long enough to truly consider the inner city. There is horror, of course, and sadness, frustration, and anger. There is fear. There is guilt, as well, and so there should be. But I hope that in these stories you will find more than just those first emotions, because surely I have found more.

I have found goodness here, for one thing, exceeding by far the goodness I presumed to bring with me when I first came. I have found excitement, too, and beauty, accomplishment, and joy. Here is hope. Here is love. Because, like everywhere, here is Jesus.

He is not named on every page of this book, just as he is not named in every moment of our lives. Yet he is always here, just the same, and often not hard to find. Jesus is the Way, the Truth, and the Life, after all, so whenever you find any one of those things, you are finding him, whether or not you recognize it. Still, to recognize it, that is, to recognize Jesus whenever and wherever he waits for you, is the essence of faith and the work and art of a disciple. For that reason, I hope most of all that you see Jesus in these stories.

I also hope they make you think.

Certainly there is plenty to think about in regard to the inner city, especially for those of us who call ourselves servants of God. Be we insiders or outsiders, it is far too easy for Christians to reduce the gospel to a trite message about personal piety or eternal security, without wrestling with the radical and holistic consequences of Jesus' life and teachings. Obviously I have offered you precious little social theory here. The best I can do is to try to share the ongoing crisis of my own faith. So, if you finish reading this book with more questions than answers, I may have succeeded, because that is precisely how I am finishing writing it.

Yet, there is the practical matter of application. That is what my friend Owen was driving at when he asked, "What am I supposed to do with a book like this?" In other words, he was asking, *Now that you have me feeling and thinking in a new way, what do you want me to do?*

If you are eighteen to twenty-nine years of age and single, then my answer is easy: Apply to join Mission Year! No matter what you plan to do with the rest of your life, you should first spend a year living and working among the poor in the inner city as a follower of Jesus, so that you can experience these things I have written about firsthand. I know I sound crazy, but let me ask you this: Knowing what you know about Jesus and the poor, why wouldn't you give a year to find out why he loves them so much?

Of course, coming to live and work for God in the inner city is not the answer for everybody. God has made each of us with different gifts and abilities, and he calls each of us to different jobs and places. However, there are some things he means for all of us to do, and first among them is loving other people.

A friend of a friend of mine once wrote to Mother Teresa, asking to go and join her in ministering to the desperately needy people of Calcutta. The wise old saint's reply was only one sentence long: "Find your own Calcutta." To which I would add, find your own inner city.

What are you supposed to do with this book?

Put it down. Open your eyes. Open your ears. Every person you met on these pages is living in your world. Some of them are waiting for you to find them, to listen to them, to offer yourself as a friend. Some are waiting to teach you something, about yourself maybe, or about God. Some of them are Jesus himself, hiding in the most unlikely people and places you or I could ever imagine. Open your life. These are my stories. Where are yours?

For more information, contact

Mission Year
990 Buttonwood Street
Philadelphia, PA 19123

1-888-340-9327

www.missionyear.org